Choices
and Constraints
in
Family Life

Choices
and Constraints
in
Family Life

Second Edition

Maureen Baker

OXFORD
UNIVERSITY PRESS

OXFORD
UNIVERSITY PRESS

8 Sampson Mews, Suite 204, Don Mills, Ontario M3C 0H5
www.oupcanada.com

Oxford University Press is a department of the University of Oxford.
It furthers the University's objective of excellence in research, scholarship,
and education by publishing worldwide in

Oxford   New York

Auckland   Cape Town   Dar es Salaam   Hong Kong   Karachi
Kuala Lumpur   Madrid   Melbourne   Mexico City   Nairobi
New Delhi   Shanghai   Taipei   Toronto

With offices in

Argentina   Austria   Brazil   Chile   Czech Republic   France   Greece
Guatemala   Hungary   Italy   Japan   Poland   Portugal   Singapore
South Korea   Switzerland   Thailand   Turkey   Ukraine   Vietnam

Oxford is a trade mark of Oxford University Press
in the UK and in certain other countries

Published in Canada
by Oxford University Press

Copyright © 2010 Oxford University Press Canada

The moral rights of the author have been asserted

Database right Oxford University Press (maker)

First Published 2010

Library and Archives Canada Cataloguing in Publication

Baker, Maureen

Choices and constraints in family life / Maureen Baker. — 2nd ed.

Includes bibliographical references and index.
ISBN 978-0-19-543159-9
1. Families—Textbooks. I. Title.
HQ519.B34 2010   306.85   C2009-906157-0

Cover image: Digital Vision Photography / Veer Images

Oxford University Press is committed to our environment.
This book is printed on Forest Stewardship Council certified paper,
harvested from a responsibly managed forest.

Mixed Sources
Product group from well-managed
forests, and other controlled sources
www.fsc.org Cert no. SW-COC-002358
FSC © 1996 Forest Stewardship Council

Printed and bound in Canada.

1 2 3 4 – 13 12 11 10

Contents

List of Tables and Figure

Tables

Figure

List of Boxes

Preface and Acknowledgements

Many young students seem to believe that they can create their own 'personal biographies' or freely develop their own individual lifestyle and domestic relationships. Although I agree that more personal choices are available now compared to a few decades ago, I argue in this book that many of the old constraints on relationships continue and some new ones have been added. Current knowledge and controversies about intimacy, the nature of marriage and family life are examined from the fields of sociology, anthropology, cultural studies, psychology, gender studies, and social history. These research findings are compared with some of the concerns of politicians and representations of family life in the media.

Over the past few decades, the study of family life has changed in terms of the basic assumptions behind the field, the issues being researched, and the practical relevance of the research. In my view, new life has been breathed into the sub-discipline by paying greater attention to gender relations and domestic work as well as issues relating to cohabitation, same-sex relationships, the creation of personal identity, new reproductive technologies, fathering, and public discourse about parenting and family responsibilities. I show that while innovative family patterns have developed in recent years, some of these 'new' patterns are really variations on older themes. In addition, a number of battles fought in the 1960s and 1970s relating to gender equity and work/family balance continue unresolved into the twenty-first century.

A number of colleagues have assisted with the development and preparation of this book. Back in the early 1980s, Professor Lorne Tepperman from the Sociology Department at the University of Toronto encouraged me to edit my first book about families by recommending me to a publisher. Lorne also recommended me to author this book with Oxford University Press. I am very grateful for both suggestions. Secondly, I would like to thank the staff at Oxford University Press, especially Allison McDonald (developmental editor) and Jessie Coffey (copy editor), who transformed my revised manuscript into the second edition. Although I live in Auckland, New Zealand, and they operate from Toronto, the process ran very smoothly using electronic mail with both editions. Thirdly, I would like to thank my partner, Dr David Tippin, for his continuing support throughout the preparation of this book and all my other academic projects.

Maureen Baker
University of Auckland
New Zealand
June 2009

Chapter 1

Conceptualizing Families

Learning Objectives

- To understand the various ways that families have been defined and studied
- To relate the conceptualization of families to theoretical frameworks used in the social sciences
- To explore the ways that family and marriage systems vary by culture, and family experiences vary by gender and social class

Chapter Outline

This chapter defines families and family policies, and discusses cultural variations in the meaning of marriage and in family experiences. The chapter also examines three major ways that academics have conceptualized family life and offers some insights into the advantages and problems of each theoretical framework, as well as various research methodologies.

Introduction

Compared to a few generations ago, some aspects of family life have changed considerably. For one thing, our intimate relationships now involve more personal choices about partners and sexual behaviour. In the twenty-first century, more of us believe that we have the right to choose our partners without interference from relatives or officials, and that we should not be forced to remain with that person if our relationship proves unsatisfactory. In addition, more people feel that whether or not they legally marry and produce children should be their own decision rather than something they might be pressured to do by family members, religious leaders, or politicians.

In this book, I argue that intimate relationships are certainly influenced by our personal preferences but to a large extent our 'choices' are shaped by family circumstances and events in the wider society, such as downturns in the economy, labour market changes, technological innovations, media representations, and new ideas about human rights or personal entitlements. Consequently, patterns are noticeable in family life, including rising rates of cohabitation among heterosexual and same-sex couples, fewer births of which more occur outside marriage, and higher rates of separation, re-partnering, and stepfamilies. In fact, similar trends are apparent in most Western industrialized countries (Lewis, 2003; Hantrais, 2004; OECD, 2007).

Although more of us insist on making our own choices about partners and children, many people also expect government or public agencies to safeguard their human rights, to protect them from violent relationships, to help them manage problem children, or to supplement their inadequate household incomes. New public expectations have heightened controversies about who is responsible for protecting and supporting vulnerable family members and those in need. Public debates have also questioned the validity of new forms of marriage, sought solutions to declining fertility and the enforcement of child support after separation, and examined new ways of interacting with immigrants whose family practices diverge from the majority.

'Child poverty' is growing in many countries despite political promises to reduce or abolish it, and this poverty is aggravated by higher rates of marriage breakdown as well as labour market deregulation (UNICEF, 2005). Especially in the 'liberal' welfare states (or Canada and the English-speaking countries), policy-makers continue to search for ways to reduce this poverty. However, they are also concerned about maximizing personal responsibility for family well-being and reducing income taxes and social spending—and one set of goals seems to counteract the other. Nevertheless, controversies over relationships and family obligations permeate both public policy debates and private conversations.

This book aims to understand how relationships and family practices have changed over the past decades in Western industrialized countries, and to differentiate between *actual* changes and the misconceptions voiced in political speeches or perpetuated in the media. Discussions of social research will reveal that our personal choices about intimate partners, having children, dissolving relationships, and maintaining contact with parents and siblings are influenced by our family and cultural upbringing, our socio-economic circumstances, the social policy environment, and political and economic events in the larger society. This means that the nature of family and personal life is always changing, although some aspects remain remarkably stable.

The studies and examples used to illustrate the arguments in this book are derived from several different countries but focus particularly on Canada and the English-speaking countries. These countries have been labelled **liberal welfare states** (Esping-Andersen, 1990) because they usually expect individuals to rely on employment earnings and the assistance of household members and voluntary organizations for well-being. Relatively ungenerous state assistance is made available only when people cannot cope. However, by examining relationships and families in various countries, eras, income levels, and cultural circumstances, we are better able to understand the diverse factors that influence personal choices about love, sex, and marriage.

Defining Families

The word 'family' is used in various ways in popular usage, referring in different contexts to our parents, siblings, spouse, and children, as well as referring to all the relatives sharing a household and the larger group of relatives with whom we maintain some contact. Social scientists usually feel the need to clarify the meaning by adding qualifiers such as **nuclear family** (husband, wife, and children sharing a household with no other adults present) or **extended family** (husband, wife, and children sharing a household with other relatives such as grandparents, aunts, or uncles). Most academic and policy definitions focus on the structure of family households—whether it is nuclear or extended, and whether it contains one or two parents. They also emphasize the legality of the relationships—whether partners are married or cohabiting—rather than considering feelings of love or obligation, or shared activities.

Early social scientists called the family a **social institution**, emphasizing the rules and expectations that guided family interaction. They stated that the family consisted of at least two adults of the opposite sex, united by marriage, living together, pooling their resources, sharing intimacy, and producing and raising children (Murdock, 1949; Goode, 1964). Over the years, this definition has been challenged as ideological, outmoded, and overemphasizing the heterosexual nuclear family. Increasingly, academics and ordinary citizens argue that the structure of families or the legality of their relationships is less meaningful and has fewer implications for their daily lives than the services that household members provide for each other or how they feel about these relationships. Consequently, both researchers and advocacy groups suggest that definitions should be broadened to encompass caring and enduring intimate relationships regardless of their legal or blood ties (Eichler, 1997; Jamieson, 1998; Smart and Neale, 1999).

Governments, however, are particularly concerned about who shares a dwelling, whether or not couples are legally married or share a 'marriage-like relationship', and the legal relationship between adults and any children living in the household. This information tells state officials who should be held accountable for financial support, care, and protection. They are particularly interested in whether households contain one or two adults, how much income is available to support the children, whether families require state income assistance, and whether vulnerable members are 'at risk'. The state develops specific definitions of family for planning and policy purposes and is unwilling to allow people to create their own definitions, especially when making decisions about entitlement for social benefits or immigration status. However, advocacy groups persistently pressure the state to expand or clarify its definition of family. Many governments have recently responded by including same-sex couples and by acknowledging stepfamilies and the extended family arrangements of immigrants or indigenous peoples.

The fact that families are ancient institutions with many structural variations provides opportunities for social scientists to note patterns and trends over time and to identify factors promoting change, or at least associated with change. For example, social researchers try to understand how couple relationships and reproductive choices vary with socio-economic transformations such as industrialization, urbanization, the expansion of the service sector of the economy, widespread migration, the global economy, the computer revolution, and a growing consumer-oriented society. Researchers and theorists study how these societal trends influence personal attitudes and behaviour, as well as public discourse, or the way people talk about sexuality, marriage, reproduction, parental responsibility, and divorce.

Despite evidence of diversity, 'the family' is still being discussed in some circles as though it were a single institution that means the same to everyone. However, there is considerable evidence that family life has always varied—parents remarried, children lived with step-parents, and family members in the past shared dissimilar views about the nature of their home life and personal relationships. Canadian sociologist Margrit Eichler (1988, 2005) argued that before the 1980s, both the academic and policy portrayal of North American families resembled the nuclear family (with male breadwinner and female caregiver) rather than any other family configuration. Assumptions about family life were conservative and often based on the views of one member, without acknowledging gender differences or variations in viewpoint between children and parents. Academics and policy-makers also normalized the experiences of young, white, middle-class families in which two heterosexual parents and their biological children shared a household without other relatives, and the parents maintained a gendered division of labour.

Opponents of same-sex marriage still promote this nuclear family model even though most people no longer live in these kinds of households in OECD countries (Lewis, 2003; Hantrais, 2004). A growing percentage of the population lives alone, some people never marry or reproduce, many couples separate, parents re-partner, children live with step-siblings, and children grow up and leave their older parent(s) in childless households. Although social research now emphasizes the multi-dimensional nature of family life, this diversity is not always incorporated into public discourse or social policy debates. In most government analyses, a 'family with children' refers to a heterosexual couple or lone parent sharing a dwelling with never-married children. These children could be their biological offspring or the children of their partner or adopted children. A lone-parent or sole-parent family usually refers to one parent who shares a dwelling with her (occasionally, his) never-married children, without another adult present in the household. Although governments sometimes call these units 'lone-parent (or sole-parent) families', in fact they are often 'lone-parent households', because the father usually maintains some contact with his children even when he lives apart. Consequently, other researchers use the concept of the 'post-divorce family' to encompass both the non-resident father (who often lives alone or with a new partner) and the mother-led household containing their children. More descriptive terms, such as same-sex families, blended families, or stepfamilies, can help to clarify vague definitions.

The most prevalent definition used in policy research is the **census family**. There are cross-national variations of this term but Statistics Canada, for example, has redefined this unit as:

> a married couple and the children, if any, of either or both spouses; a couple living common law and the children, if any, of either or both partners; or, a lone parent of any marital status with at least one child living in the same dwelling and that child or those children. All members of a particular census family live in the same dwelling. A couple may be of opposite or same sex. Children may be children by birth, marriage or adoption regardless of their age or marital status as long as they live in the dwelling and do not have their own spouse or child living in the dwelling. Grandchildren living with their grandparent(s) but with no parents present also constitute a census family. (Statistics Canada, 2006)

Some cultural or religious groups prefer to live in extended family households consisting of their parents and/or siblings, as well as their spouse and children. These groups argue that the 'census family' is only one family structure (essentially the nuclear family or a one-parent household) and that to assume this is the normal arrangement misrepresents sources of caring and social support in their lives. This definition also creates problems when they want to sponsor family members as immigrants, especially their unmarried adult daughters or married siblings. Using a nuclear family definition could also create a problem if a large group of extended family wanted to visit a sick household member in hospital but were denied access because they were not 'close family'. Assuming that the normal family is nuclear also implies that the family relationships of same-sex couples are different and less valid, and it deprives them of certain social benefits such as the right to be considered 'next of kin' in medical emergencies. Issues of entitlement are always contentious, but a clear definition of 'family' is essential in establishing eligibility for social benefits or for designing the government census or a research project.

In this book, I use the plural term 'families' to reinforce the idea that variations have always been apparent and that families were never as uniform as some people have implied. Generally, my definition of families is similar to the census definition plus the extended family (with grandparents or aunts/uncles).

However, I acknowledge that definitions need to be more specific for some purposes, especially those relating to the eligibility for social benefits, and I often use adjectives with 'family' to specify meaning (such as 'step-family').

Defining 'Family Policies'

Various family policies are also discussed in this book, which are defined as official decisions to implement state-sponsored social programs, services, regulations, and laws that specifically affect families with children. These policies might relate to reproductive health, family well-being, or the maintenance of family income. They could also enforce financial or caring obligations among family members, protect vulnerable family members from harm or neglect, or enable the integration of employment and caring work. Family programs do not have to be delivered directly by the state but they must be mandated or regulated by the state to be included in my definition. Therefore, programs contracted out to voluntary agencies or subsidized by public money could be included, such as child welfare services contracted to the Children's Aid Society or to an indigenous tribal group. Employer-sponsored programs for maternity leave or for family responsibilities also are included in the definition of **family policy** because governments often require employers to provide these benefits or their provision is required by international agreements among countries (Baker, 2006).

When academics or politicians talk about the **state**, they usually are referring to legislative and executive bodies (such as parliament and government departments) as well as the publicly funded agencies (such as child welfare) mandated to implement or enforce these policies. When studying family policies, the concept of **welfare state** refers to the social services and income support programs designed to improve the social and economic well-being of families and to regulate and control family and personal life. Researchers and theorists studying the development of welfare states have shown that nations differ in the ways they think about the nature of family life and social provision, the kinds of programs they actually create, and their preferences for funding and delivering social programs.

The welfare state was generally developed between the 1940s and 1970s, when social and family life differed substantially from the present, but new social programs continue to be established and existing ones are modified. Although most have been amended since they were developed, some programs still imply that marital relationships and paid employment remain stable throughout life. Some public discourse about families also suggests that most people river live in nuclear family units consisting of a breadwinner father who supports 'his dependants' in full-time paid work and a homemaker mother who cares for the children at home or works part-time. The couple is often assumed to be heterosexual, legally married for life, and living with their two or three children who are biologically related to both parents (Eichler, 1997). However, most people no longer live this way.

Table 1.1 shows family trends from 1986 to 2006 in Canada, Australia, and New Zealand. The data indicate that fewer couples lived with children, more were cohabiting, and more households were led by lone parents in 2006. In addition, a rising percentage of couples live with stepchildren, although this is not shown in the table. If policy-makers acknowledged the degree of instability in some people's personal relationships and work patterns, the social programs they create or restructure might look quite different.

Academics have compared various countries and categorized them according to the generosity of their social provision and the philosophy underlying it. A number of categorizations exist but Canada and the United States have usually been linked together with the English-speaking countries and labelled as 'liberal' or 'residual' welfare states, meaning that in these countries individuals and families are normally assumed to be responsible for their own economic and social well-being (Esping-Andersen, 1996; O'Connor et al., 1999). Parents are held responsible for the care and support of their children both when they live together and if they separate, and spouses are expected to support and assist each other during marriage. When state benefits are made available, they are

Table 1.1 Percentage of Census Family Types, 1986 and 2006

% of All Census Families	Canada		Australia		New Zealand	
	1986	2006	1986	2006	1986	2006
Couple families with children in household	52	41	56	45	53	42
Couple families without children in household	—	43	30	37	33	40
% of couples not legally married	7	16	6	15	12	18
One-parent households	13	16	8	16	14	18

Source: Statistics Canada, 2008. 'Census Snapshop of Canada—Families', *Canadian Social Trends*, 39. Catalogue no. 11–008; AIFS, 2008; Qu and Weston, 2008; Research New Zealand, 2007: 9; Ambert, 2005; Statistics NZ, 'Family Types', 2004; NZ 1991 Census, Table 13, Family Types 1986–1991.

relatively ungenerous and well below minimum wages, even below accepted poverty levels.

In contrast, the **social democratic welfare states**, such as Sweden and Denmark, view children's well-being as a social responsibility as well as a parental one, and place more importance on redistributing income, preventing poverty, and promoting gender equity. **Corporatist welfare states** such as France and Germany—so called because they involve business, labour, and the state working together as corporate entities to create **social insurance** programs—are financed through employer and employee contributions, and are designed to replace lost wages due to unemployment, sickness, work-related injury, or retirement (Esping-Andersen, 1990). These social insurance programs were developed by trade unions, employers' groups, and government to share the cost of income loss, and they continue to be managed by representatives from these three groups.

Some theorists have argued that Australia and New Zealand should not be included with the liberal states but should instead be classified as 'wage earners' welfare states' (Castles and Shirley, 1996). These countries used to be different because their trade unions and governments sought to ensure that (male) wages were high enough to support families at a comfortable level through centralized bargaining and restrictions on immigrant labour. State assistance was also provided for home ownership but the basic income support programs targeted to low-income households were less important than these other factors to family well-being. Increasingly, however, Australia and especially New Zealand resemble the other liberal welfare states (Lunt, O'Brien, and Stephens, 2008).

Social support for families with children clearly varies cross-nationally (Hantrais, 2004; OECD, 2005b). However, important differences are also apparent among the various jurisdictions of the same country. Federal states like Canada and the United States have decentralized many social programs, which are designed and administered at the provincial or state level. In Canada, for example, the federal government retains jurisdiction over some income support programs (such as Old Age Security, Canada Pension Plan, and Employment Insurance), federal tax concessions for families, maternity/parental benefits, and divorce law. The provinces have jurisdiction over marriage law, **maternity leave** provisions, social services such as child protection, child-care services, health-care services, education, and social assistance. They also control the division of matrimonial property upon separation of spouses, and laws pertaining to the implementation of child custody, access, child support, and spousal support (Guest, 1997; McGilly, 1998). In addition, some Canadian provinces, such as Ontario, allow municipalities to create and administer child-care provisions and income support for some categories of welfare recipients.

Divided jurisdiction within a federal state permits inconsistencies to develop among different regions and inhibits the creation of national programs in matters of provincial jurisdiction (Baker, 2006). This means that 'the welfare state' might not be internally consistent in its goals or in eligibility rules for benefits, even within the same country and the same kind of social policy. In addition, some jurisdictions might provide generous social provision for retired people but restrict support for children or employed mothers. This suggests that studies of 'the' welfare state might fruitfully be broken down into jurisdictions as well as particular policy areas, such as employment benefits or family-related programs.

Gender, Social Class, and Family Policies

State involvement in families varies by gender and social class as well as by jurisdiction. Women's access to social provision has been shaped by their relationship to men and children, their incomes, by different views about suitable roles for women and mothers, and by prevalent models of the typical family (Lewis, 1992; Sainsbury, 1993; Leira, 2002). Men are assumed to be the main breadwinners and women the primary care providers within the liberal and corporatist welfare states, and parents are seen as fully responsible for their own children. In addition, men tend to receive more generous benefits through paid work rather than parenthood, while women gain their entitlement mainly as mothers and wives. In contrast, the social democratic states tend to view both marriage partners as earners and carers. They see the well-being of children as a joint responsibility between parents and the state, exemplified by the provision of affordable child care and generous social provision for leave for family responsibilities.

Historically, liberal welfare states have treated low-income wives and widows as more deserving of state income support than never-married or separated mothers. If women became lone mothers through premarital pregnancy, separation, or divorce, they used to be offered minimal benefits (Ursel, 1992; Baker and Tippin, 1999). These benefits were sometimes delivered in discretionary ways by welfare officials rather than being seen as legal entitlements. The recipients were thought to require close scrutiny concerning their maternal and moral behaviour to ensure that they were truly eligible and not defrauding the taxpayers (Swift, 1995; Little, 1998). In contrast, wives and widows often became eligible for more income support through the husband's work-related social insurance entitlements as well as his private insurance policies. Now, the benefits available for lone mothers vary less by their route to lone parenthood, but married women and widows are still more likely to gain access to private insurance or pension funds acquired through their male partners' earnings.

Men typically receive benefits from employers or the state as earners rather than husbands or fathers. Work-related benefits may be sponsored by employers but some are financed through social insurance programs, such as Canada's Employment Insurance. Receiving such benefits involves less investigation into recipients' personal lives and higher payments based on the contributions from employees and employers (Sainsbury, 1993, 1996). As more women enter full-time paid work, they also become eligible for employment-related benefits, but women earn lower average wages and make lower contributions to social insurance programs, and therefore receive lower average benefits than men. If they privately insure their earnings or their life, the final payment also reflects lower female earnings as well as their longer life expectancy.

State intervention has also varied by social class and ethnicity. Welfare workers have been permitted to investigate the family circumstances and living conditions of impoverished families even though such investigations would be considered an infringement of privacy for those with higher incomes. For example, a lone mother living on social assistance might be visited by social workers searching for evidence of another adult living in her home who might be considered a potential breadwinner (Little, 1998). The state has been most interventionist with visible minorities and indigenous peoples. In the past, impoverished but much-loved children from indigenous families were considered to be 'at risk' of maltreatment, disease, and lack of education by well-intentioned missionaries and government officials (Baker, 2001b). Consequently, these children used to be removed from their parental homes and placed in residential schools run by churches or the government, often against the wishes both of the children and of their parents. Since the 1960s, these practices have ceased because they are considered racist and psychologically damaging, although the 'Sixties Scoop' in Canada resulted in thousands of Aboriginal children from impoverished or dysfunctional families being placed in foster care and adopted into non-Aboriginal families (Dickason, 2006: 229). Today, income support programs and local schools have been developed, efforts are made to keep children from problem homes within their own communities, and local child welfare services are sometimes managed by the indigenous people themselves.

This discussion suggests that state involvement in family life changes over time because policy ideas and social programs originate from different governments with varying agendas, and that ideas about human rights and the role of the state in family life evolve over the years. In addition, policy reform tends to be incremental and developed from previous programs, because it is easier in a democracy to make minor modifications to existing policy than to introduce major reforms.

Researchers have also studied family life in different cultures, investigating the connections among family structure, patterns of authority, marriage systems, descent and residence rules, and how cross-cultural variations relate to systems of economic production, religious beliefs, and other cultural patterns. Academics have questioned whether or not the nuclear family is a universal group, whether men are always family 'heads', and what difference it makes when the marriage system permits more than one spouse at a time. One of the central debates has been whether or not the nuclear family is a product of industrialization, urbanization, and westernization. If so, will families begin to look more similar around the world if westernization and global culture expand? In the next section, some of these issues will be outlined as I discuss cultural variations in family patterns.

Cultural Variations in Families

Family Structure

When people in Western industrialized countries live in family households, they usually form nuclear families consisting of a husband, wife, and their children sharing a dwelling without other relatives present. Some academics assume that, in the past, most households in both Western and non-Western societies consisted of extended families in which several generations shared a residence. They believe that more people came to live in nuclear families with the pressures of **industrialization** and urban migration between the seventeenth and the nineteenth centuries.

In France, Frédéric Le Play (1806–82) studied changes in the rural European 'stem family', an extended family consisting of parents and one married son who would eventually inherit the family property. He lamented the rise of the 'unstable' nuclear family and the demise of patriarchal authority caused by industrialization and modernization. Friedrich Engels (1884) also saw the nuclear family as the product of industrialization, theorizing about the ways that society and family structure were transformed from the times when people lived in large hunting-and-gathering clans or kin groups through to private nuclear families in the industrial cities of England. American sociologists Parsons and Bales (1955) were also concerned about the loss of the extended family, which they felt provided more effective authority, household labour, child care, companionship, and economic security than the nuclear family.

Social historians have demonstrated, however, that nuclear family households were always the most typical living arrangements both in Europe and among the European colonists (Laslett, 1971; Goldthorpe, 1987). One reason that this living arrangement persisted is that life expectancies were much shorter than today and many parents died before their children married. In the colonies, extended family households were even less common among Europeans because many of these settlers had left their parents and older relatives behind when they migrated. Canadian sociologist Emily Nett (1981) contended that it had never been a widespread practice for married couples to live with their parents at any time in the Canadian history of European settlement. Class differences are also apparent as lower-income families with British backgrounds were more likely than richer settlers to share accommodation with parents and children, especially in times of financial need, separation, or widowhood.

Despite the prevalence of nuclear families in the English-speaking countries, extended families continue to be more prevalent among many indigenous peoples (Baker, 2001b). In addition, extended families continue to serve as living arrangements and support groups in parts of Africa, South Asia, and the Middle East. They have become slightly more prevalent in high-immigration countries such as Australia, Canada, New Zealand, and the United States as they accept more immigrants from countries with extended-family systems. In Canada, the percentage of three-generation households increased from 1986 to 1996, mainly as a result of increased Asian immigration, but only three per cent of households included three generations in 1996 (Che-Alford and Hamm, 1999). In the 2006 census, about 1.3 per cent of people lived with relatives in family households that could approximate an extended family (Statistics Canada, 2007). This suggests that most Canadians consider living alone more acceptable and feasible, and that many cultural groups alter their traditional practices after migration.

Practical constraints as well as cultural traditions influence family structure and living arrangements. Immigrants with few economic resources and limited skills in the host country's official language are more likely to share accommodation than wealthier immigrants who can afford separate housing, those who can communicate more effectively, and those able to find employment (Thomas, 2001). Furthermore, living with relatives is not necessarily permanent but could involve sharing accommodation with adult siblings until separate housing can be located or financed. Living with relatives is more prevalent among female immigrants, those with lower education and incomes, and recent arrivals (ibid, 21).

This suggests that gender, social class, and culture (as well as personal choice) influence whether immigrants continue to live in extended families. Immigrants often attempt to integrate into the new country by giving up some aspects of their cultural practices. This means that the family demography of the second generation tends to look more like that of others born in that country (Albanese, 2009). In other countries, especially in rural areas or those with few Western influences, cultural traditions strongly influence marriage and family patterns, and the decisions of elders might override the personal choices of youth.

Authority and Lineage

Most family systems around the world designate a 'head' to make family decisions and represent the group to the larger community and state authorities. In both Western and non-Western societies, the oldest male typically is the family head, and this system, called **patriarchy**, has a long tradition that permeates laws and practices around the world. In the liberal welfare states, families were legally patriarchal in the past, but these countries have reformed their laws and practices and no longer assume that men officially lead the family (Kamerman and Kahn, 1997). In fact, Western states have been pressured to eliminate most remnants of patriarchy and to create legal equality between men and women, both within the household and in the larger society. However, vestiges of patriarchy are still apparent, such as the practice of fathers 'giving away' their daughters to the groom during some traditional marriage ceremonies.

Matriarchy is an authority system in which women are granted more authority than men, but such systems are rare throughout the world. At the time of European contact, the Iroquois tribes of North America were described as matriarchal because women's power in the economy, politics, religious ceremonies, and family life exceeded that of women in French and English cultures, as well as women in other Native tribes (Brown, 1988). In the 1930s, the American anthropologist Margaret Mead referred to the Tchambuli people of New Guinea as matriarchal because women seemed to run the economy and make most practical decisions while men were engaged in cultural pursuits (Mead, 1935). Working-class black families in the Caribbean and the United States have been called matriarchal, or at least **matrifocal**, because so many of these households are led by lone mothers while the fathers live elsewhere, or the mother/wife is the pivotal figure in many of these two-parent families (Smith, 1996). For a society or family to be considered matriarchal, women must hold considerable respect, decision-making authority, and control over household resources (Sanday, 2002).

Some sociologists and anthropologists have argued that laws and unwritten rules guide behaviour within and between families in all societies. Family law designates certain categories of people as 'out of bounds' for sex and marriage but cultural traditions also govern family behaviour. For example, patterns of descent may determine where newly married couples live, how they address family members, what surname their children will receive, and from whom they inherit. When people marry, they may also be encouraged to grant more importance to their relationships with one set of parents or siblings, as we will see in the next section.

Marriage Systems

In many cultures, marriages are arranged by elders, as we will discuss in more detail in Chapter 3. In these arrangements, close intimate relationships between the couple are not priorities because marriage represents a union between extended families rather than individuals. Young people are encouraged to want to marry in order to acquire adult status, to augment their position in the community through parenthood, to gain satisfaction from watching their children mature, to continue the family name, and eventually to become respected elders within their family and community. In cultures where the inheritance of wealth and the continuity of kin lines and family name are important, arranged marriages or partially arranged marriages remain widespread. Young people sometimes appreciate family assistance with the difficult task of finding a compatible life partner who meets their relatives' expectations. They may justify parental assistance by the high divorce rate among Western or free-choice marriages, which suggests that young people who make their own decisions often make ill-informed ones that they later regret. Furthermore, many immigrants and indigenous people guard their family practices as part of their cultural identity that they are unwilling to shed.

It is still legal in many parts of the world for a man to marry more than one wife at a time if he has the resources to support them. In the 1990s, three-quarters of the world's societies still preferred **polygyny**, or multiple wives for one husband (Saxton, 1993), although the percentage actually living in these unions was lower. Polygyny continues to be practised in some African countries as well as some in Southern and Western Asia, especially those using Islamic law. In sub-Saharan Africa, about half of married women aged 15–49 were in polygynous unions in Benin, Burkina Faso, and Guinea, and over 40 per cent in Mali, Senegal, and Togo in the 1990s (UN, 2000: 28). Wealthy men are more likely than those with fewer resources to take on more than one legal wife (Broude, 1994).

Polygynous unions tend to be associated with patriarchal authority and wider age gaps between husbands and wives. They are more common among rural and less-educated women, as well as those who do not formally work for pay outside the household (UN, 2000: 28). Multiple wives, who are sometimes sisters, may resent their husband taking a new partner, but they may also welcome her assistance with household work, child care, and horticulture, and may value her companionship in a society where marriage partners are seldom close friends. Furthermore, the husband's second marriage typically elevates the rank of the first wife, who then becomes the supervisor of the younger wife's household work. However, family conflict can occur among the children of different wives, who may also see less of their father than children from monogamous marriages (Al-Krenawi et al., 2008).

Polygamy refers to the practice of having more than one spouse at a time, but polygyny is much more prevalent than **polyandry**, which is marriage between one woman and several husbands. When polyandry does occur, the husbands are often brothers (fraternal polyandry) and the practice may relate to the need to keep land in one parcel (Ihinger-Tallman and Levinson, 2003). However, most societies prefer polygyny because more children can be born into marriages with multiple wives and this could be important if children are the main source of labour for the family or community. Also, the identification of the father is particularly important in **patrilineal** societies because children receive their father's surname, belong to his kin group, and inherit from him, and married men are responsible for supporting their children. Knowing who the father is would be difficult with multiple husbands, so this is not usually an acceptable form of marriage in patrilineal systems. Most societies have been patriarchal and men more often have the power to ensure that the marriage system suits their own interests.

All westernized countries have prohibited polygamy. Judeo-Christian beliefs promote sexual exclusivity. Some explain these doctrines on the assumption that men would experience difficulty providing adequate financial and emotional support for more than one wife. However, some groups have practised polygamy in nineteenth- and twentieth-century North America, including some Mormons in Utah and British Columbia, but the general population strongly objected and insisted that the authorities put a stop to this practice. In New Zealand, some Maori tribes practised polygyny at the time of European contact, but the Christian missionaries and British settlers opposed the practice and ensured that it did not continue (Baker, 2001b).

Although polygamy is now against the law in all the liberal welfare states, it may continue to exist clandestinely in some communities where a man has one legal wife but also cohabits with other women. Neighbours or state officials might not interfere because they assume that these other women are room-mates or relatives rather than wives, or may feel that their neighbours' sexual relations are not their business. In addition, some men who travel for a living have maintained female partners who are unknown to each other. However, this is neither legal nor socially acceptable in Western countries.

Some new immigrants come from countries accepting polygamous marriage. This could lead to problems for immigration departments of receiving countries unless they develop clear policies about how polygamous marriage should be treated in terms of legal recognition, support obligations, and inheritance rights. The receiving country can certainly refuse to permit new polygamous arrangements as well as potential immigrants with existing polygamous marriages. If it permits entry to men with partners back home and refuses to recognize their previous legal obligations, official wives and legitimate children could be left destitute when their husbands emigrate (Beeby, 2006).

Group marriage also continues to exist but in Western industrialized countries it is illegal and socially unacceptable. Historically, it was practised in some utopian communities, such as the Oneida Community in nineteenth-century New York State or more recent communal experiments in the 1960s. In these marriages, more than one couple consider themselves married to one another, and they share resources, meals, child-rearing, and sexual access. However, these arrangements tend to last only a few years, partly due to opposition from the authorities, but also as a result of interpersonal conflicts (Ihinger-Tallman and Levinson, 2003).

People in westernized countries are permitted to marry only one partner at a time, although an increasing percentage of the population divorce and subsequently remarry or cohabit without any social or legal ceremony. However, even when couples initially live together without a wedding, many legally marry later when they make a long-term commitment to each other or when they decide to have children. Among these, many participate in formal wedding ceremonies and celebrations with the traditional cultural symbols of virginity, fertility, and patriarchy.

At the time of marriage, most family systems require the exchange of gifts. Time-consuming negotiations as well as traditional practices may guide families when they select these gifts, which may be distributed or consumed in formal ceremonies. Some cultures require families to provide dowries as part of the marriage settlement, which I discuss in more detail in Chapter 3, but these practices are most often retained in rural areas where wives lack formal education or do not work for pay. When women acquire Western education and become self-supporting, they or their families are less likely to participate in arranged marriages, dowry negotiations, or polygamous marriages.

Multiculturalism and Cultural Clashes

With high immigration rates in countries such as Australia, Canada, New Zealand, and the United States, more people are becoming aware of variations in family patterns, although they may not accept them as normal, acceptable, or fair. A number of contentious practices relate to the status of girls and women. Female circumcision, for example, is practised in some cultures to discourage non-marital sexual activity among women. However, the United Nations, many Western governments, and women's groups have viewed this practice as unacceptable, a violation of human rights, and a risk to women's health and well-being.

Prenatal screening is routinely done for pregnant women in most Western countries but in some cultural communities it has included the selective abortion of female fetuses. Males are still preferred in some cultures because they are granted higher status, continue the family lineage, financially support the extended family, and bring wealth in the form of wedding gifts or marriage settlements. Selective abortions are prohibited in Western countries but they continue to occur because abortions can sometimes be performed in private clinics or with less official scrutiny. The United Nations and state authorities have tried to reduce the preference for male babies by attempting to eliminate all forms of discrimination against girls and women, including making the dowry system illegal in some countries.

Another controversial issue has been the veiling of Muslim women, a religious practice that requires women to cover their hair with a scarf when in the presence of unrelated males. Women's arms and legs are also covered with long sleeves and long dresses or trousers, and sometimes their entire bodies, including their faces, are enrobed beneath a 'burqa'. France recently outlawed the wearing of religious symbols in state schools, angering the Muslim community by requiring their schoolgirls to remove their headscarves during lessons.

In 2004, two Muslim refugee women living in New Zealand were asked to serve as Crown witnesses in an insurance fraud trial (Devereux, 2004). The women wanted to remain veiled during their court appearance, but the lawyer for the accused man successfully argued against their request. He stated that the court and his client are entitled to see the faces of witnesses in order to help verify their verbal statements by observing their demeanour or body language. The women refused to remove their burqas in court and one claimed that she would rather kill herself than show her face in public. Religious leaders were consulted, who stated that the burqa was not required by the Koran but was simply a religious custom exemplifying female modesty in the company of unrelated males. The New Zealand authorities subsequently asked these women to remove their veils but permitted them to give evidence behind a screen so that the male public could not observe them during the trial.

These examples, as well as discussions about structural variations in family systems, shed some light on the cultural relativity of personal beliefs and family practices. They also suggest a close association between family practices and religion, educational attainment, urban/rural residence, patterns of authority, and factors relating to work and economic production in the larger society. The above section has also underlined the importance of different and sometimes contradictory explanations for the existence and maintenance of family patterns, which I address below.

Conceptualizing Family Patterns

A social scientific approach to family studies is based on the assumption that intimate relationships and family practices do not occur in random ways and do not result merely from personal choices. Instead, attitudes, desires, and behaviours are influenced by family experiences, gender, culture, religion, and socio-economic circumstances in ways that create noticeable patterns. Three broad conceptual approaches are used here to analyze and explain family patterns in the social sciences. The first approach argues that social structure,   including the economy, policies, laws, and social expectations, influences and constrains family life, and alters our intimate relationships. The second argues that psychosexual development and interpersonal interaction shape personal identity and future family relationships. The third approach emphasizes the importance of prevailing ideas and cultural images in creating desires and moulding attitudes and behaviour. Understanding these conceptual frameworks can shed light on the history of ideas, the development of sociology as a discipline, and continuing academic debates about the crucial influences on social behaviour.

Structural Theories of Family Patterns

Researchers and theorists have argued since the nineteenth century that transformations in the larger society alter family life. We already mentioned the research studies of the rural European family by Le Play, considered the pioneer of empirical sociology, who argued that socio-economic changes such as urbanization and industrialization led to the rise of the nuclear family and to the demise of patriarchal authority and family hierarchy. Despite the conservative biases in his analysis, Le Play helped legitimize the study of family structure and social history (Gilding, 1997: 46).

Friedrich Engels (1820–95) also studied the impact of transformations such as urbanization and industrialization in the economy on family structure and authority patterns in England. He argued that changes in the political and economic basis of society from feudalism to capitalism altered family life by moving production outside households and into factories. These production changes encouraged a patriarchal family structure in which men, as household wage-earners, became the intermediaries between their families and the larger community, while their wives were expected to care for the children and home. As wives played a reduced role in economic production, Engels noted that their status and authority declined because society increasingly measured personal worth by earning capacity (Engels, 1884). Family research using this 'political economy' perspective has continued until the present, emphasizing the ways that labour market restructuring and the development of the global economy alter family income, living arrangements, and relationships.

Political economists also argue that people's access to wealth, production, and power influences their desires, beliefs, and behaviour. In this approach, interpersonal relations, community stability, and social cohesion are de-emphasized. The focus, instead, remains on the impact of historical trends in paid and unpaid work on family structure, different life chances based on social class, and the influence of social policies on family and personal life. Historically, political economists attributed greater importance to **social class** than to gender, sexual orientation, age, ethnicity, or race. In recent years, however, many feminist scholars have used a political economy perspective, acknowledging the importance of gender, social class, and race to the kinds of work people are forced to accept, their living standards, and their family relationships (Luxton and Corman, 2001; Bezanson, 2006).

Another structural approach, **structural functionalism**, argues that 'the family' is the basic 'social institution' of society, containing rules, expected forms of behaviour, and hierarchical relationships. The family influences social stability because it ideally offers emotional support, companionship, sexual expression, reproduction, and the socialization of children. This institution also provides important functions for the larger society by maintaining social order and control through the disciplining of children and other family members. The extended family especially offers protection from outsiders, while individuals often relate to the outside world through their family head. Families usually co-operate financially and help each other through hard times by sharing resources. Finally, people acquire money and property through inheritance from family members, which suggests that social status and wealth are largely established and perpetuated through families.

European anthropologists, such as Bronislaw Malinowski (1884–1942) and Alfred Radcliffe-Brown (1881–1955), used a structural functional approach to compare culture and family life in various parts of the world, including the South Pacific and Australia. They studied how family systems were integrated into the entire culture. Later, the American Margaret Mead (1901–78) became one of the first female anthropologists to carry out field research among South Pacific cultures and focused primarily on how cultural expectations and practices influenced girls as they matured into women. The ideas of these researchers were very influential and widely debated among academics and educated citizens at the time.

Throughout the 1950s and 1960s, American sociologist Talcott Parsons (1902–79) and his collaborator Robert Bales theorized about family life from a structural functionalist perspective. Focusing on the American family, they concluded that industrialization and urbanization produce a smaller and relatively isolated nuclear family that specializes in the socialization of children and in meeting the personal needs of family members (Thorne, 1982: 7). They assumed that the family as an institution has two basic structures: a hierarchy of generations in which children are expected to obey their parents, and a differentiation of adults into instrumental and expressive **roles**. Parsons and Bales made the debatable argument that the wife necessarily takes the expressive role or maintains social relations and cares for others, while the husband assumes the instrumental role or earns the money for the family and deals with the outside world (ibid.).

Present-day structural functionalists now acknowledge that gender roles have changed but some continue to imply that a certain type of family structure (male breadwinner/female homemaker) was maintained throughout history because it was 'functional for society' when it may have been functional mainly for heterosexual men or for capitalism (ibid.). Functionalists still talk about 'the family' as though there is one acceptable family form rather than many variations. They also believe that behaviour is largely determined by social expectations, rules, and family upbringing and therefore not easily altered through personal choice. Change is sometimes considered to be disruptive rather than normal, and individual opposition to social pressure has been viewed as 'deviance'. Consequently, the structural functionalists do not deal with social change and conflict as well as the political economists, and neither focuses on the dynamic nature of interpersonal relations or sees the individual as the agent of social change.

A variation of structural functionalism is **systems theory**, which views the family as a social system. Family members are seen as interdependent and any change in the behaviour of one member affects the others. The family is also seen as a task-performing unit that is expected to meet the requirements of both the larger society and its own internal needs (Cheal, 1991: 65). The family is also a relatively closed boundary-maintaining unit that closes ranks against outside interference, as well as being an adaptive organization that incorporates new forms of behaviour and attitudes from the outside world. Family systems theory has enjoyed influence in several disciplines such as psychiatry and family therapy because it focuses attention on interrelationships within families (Braithwaite and Baxter, 2005). This has enabled therapists to assist clients to co-operate in order to enhance couple communication and to work towards positive change. However, emphasizing social interaction leaves no way of explaining why some clients exhibit certain kinds of problems more than others (Cheal, 1991: 82). Furthermore, the analysis cannot adequately explain change over time, is limited to one culture, and often focuses on one family. Viewing the family as an open system takes into consideration the external influences on family interaction but the systems approach does not focus on the social, economic, or political context within which families live.

Structural approaches may emphasize change and conflict (as does the political economy approach) or focus on consensus and cohesion (structural functionalism). However, both versions suggest that personal choices about relationships and family practices are limited by societal constraints such as access to money and power, the enforcement of regulations and rules, and social expectations about behaviour. Structuralists emphasize that we are all born into families that are part of a larger culture with existing social traditions, legal and educational systems, and expected patterns of behaviour. We cannot choose our parents or family circumstances. Some children are privileged from the beginning while others must struggle to grow up and fend for themselves under difficult circumstances. Although structuralists acknowledge that life involves personal choices, they tend to argue that 'life chances' as well as attitudes and patterns of behaviour are more often shaped by forces beyond the individual.

Interpersonal Factors Shape Family Life

In contrast to the structural approaches, other social theorists have focused on early family experiences that influence our personal identity, our attachments to parents and siblings, and intimate relationships throughout life. For example, Sigmund Freud (1856–1939) believed as a result of practising as a psychotherapist that the early years of a child's life are critical for the development of sexual identity, personality, and the ability to form lasting relationships. He argued that children are influenced by reactions to their physiology and to early interaction with parents, including the ways they are held, fed, toilet trained, talked to, listened to, and disciplined. Personality development is largely influenced by unconscious motives and repressed emotions but the Western process of socialization involves teaching children to control their selfish urges. Freud also observed that children learn partly by identifying with their same-sex parent (Baker, 2001b).

Freud's psychoanalytic theories have been criticized because his research was based almost exclusively on a clinical sample, and because he 'explained' women's 'fantasies' by portraying them as 'defective men' who subconsciously envy men's power, symbolized by their penises. Freud also assumed that socialization takes place only in early childhood but social scientists later concluded that it continues throughout life. Nevertheless, Freud made a major impact on Western thought and is credited with useful insights into personality development that stimulated further research and theorizing. Psychoanalysis was initially rejected by early feminists such as Kate Millet (1970), but it was modified and developed by Juliet Mitchell (1974) and Nancy Chodorow (1978, 1989), who used Freudian theory to analyze patriarchal society (Humm, 1995: 102). Judith Butler's theorizing about gender and sexuality has also relied heavily on psychoanalysis (Butler, 1997).

Another developmental approach was initiated in the 1920s and 1930s by the Swiss psychologist Jean Piaget, who studied systematic patterns of change occurring in children's thought processes as they mature. Like psychoanalytic theorists, Piaget suggested that all children pass through similar stages of cognitive development, but he concluded that they could not learn particular tasks or concepts until they had reached a certain level in their development. He further theorized that children's experiences and interpretations of the physical and social world modify the timing of these stages, as children actively participate in their own socialization (Baker, 2001b). In the 1960s, Erik Erikson (1963, 1968) argued that children pass through stages of development or preoccupation in which they must resolve certain crucial life issues in order to reach maturity. These include developing a capacity for trust, autonomy from parents, initiative, industry, identity, and intimacy.

Psychoanalytic theory and **developmental theory** remain influential but learning theory became a popular way of explaining child development from the 1920s to the 1980s, especially in the United States. Learning theory emphasized the importance of 'nurture' in the debate as to whether inherited characteristics ('nature') or social learning ('nurture') plays a more important role in personality and social development. According to learning theory, parents and care providers retain almost infinite potential to shape infants' attitudes and behaviour and to socialize children through rewards or punishments. Children also learn from observing and imitating adults, especially their parents and siblings. These above approaches, which tend to be psychological rather than sociological, downplay the political and socio-economic context of family life. They also suggest that adult behaviour is difficult to understand and modify without some knowledge of the early interaction experiences with parents, siblings, and other family members.

Social interaction is also the focus of the social construction or **symbolic interaction perspective**, which remains prevalent in sociology. This approach assumes that social life is determined neither by social structure nor early psychological experiences but is constructed by individual 'actors' who create their own reality through their interactions with others in families, schools, and workplaces (Berger and Luckmann, 1967). This theoretical perspective originated with the work of Americans Charles H. Cooley (1864–1929) and George Herbert Mead (1863–1931), who separately studied childhood socialization, how children develop an identity, and the importance of family interaction in this process. They noted that, early in life, parents communicate with their children through words but also through gestures, facial expressions, and tones of voice. Symbolic communication alters behaviour as individuals interpret these messages about themselves and their world. Within this perspective, the ways that children and young people interpret non-verbal communication from 'significant others' are more important than parental rules or social expectations for the development of personal identity and future relationships.

How people treat us and react to us can be influenced by the image we project, including our demeanour, dress, posture, and speech, which sociologist Erving Goffman (1959) called the 'presentation of self'. **Social constructionism** argues that the interpretation of reactions to us is critical in shaping our personalities, as a strong association exists between the development of self and what we believe others think of us (Cooley, 1902; Mead, 1934). In addition, part of growing up and becoming a social being requires developing the ability to look at the world through the eyes of others and to anticipate a particular role before taking it (anticipatory socialization). According to this theory, socialization takes place throughout the life cycle rather than only in early childhood.

Social constructionist research is often centred on what individuals and society perceive to be real or important, such as what constitutes a good relationship or a social problem (Giddens, 2006: 152; Holstein and Miller, 2006). Researchers using this perspective analyse how people come to these conclusions. They argue that it is not enough to observe people's behaviour; we also must understand why they behave that way, how they interpret their own actions, how they *feel* about what they do, and why they feel this way. In other words, perceptions and 'definitions of the situation' influence actions or behaviour, a perspective that could be seen as the precursor of post-structuralist theory, which is discussed later in this chapter.

Social exchange theory, which uses economic analogies from cost–benefit analysis to explain human behaviour, is also derived from symbolic interactionism.

The German sociologist Georg Simmel (1858–1918) argued that all human inter-actions involve some form of social exchange even when they appear to be altru-istic, and he emphasized the importance of reciprocity in everyday life. His work was translated into English during the 1950s and became influential in American sociological theory. In 1961, the American sociologist George Homans (1910–89) argued that values and norms govern behaviour but that people also attempt to minimize costs and maximize benefits when interacting with others.

Within social exchange theory, the anticipation of a 'reward', such as social approval or emotional security, motivates social behaviour. All interpersonal behaviour, including deciding on a dating or marriage partner or accepting a household division of labour, is assumed to involve a process of negotiation and bargaining (Scanzoni, 1982). Social exchange theory has been used to explain why some relationships break up and others last. When one partner feels that he or she contributes more time or emotional energy to a relationship, feel-ings of resentment may develop and he or she may start looking elsewhere for gratification.

Theoretical approaches that focus on social interaction can provide insights into the dynamics and satisfactions of relationships but cannot explain the historical or cultural change in family patterns. Nevertheless, the social con-structionist approach is widely used in sociology and gender studies, suggest-ing that social reality or collective perceptions and beliefs are more important in shaping behaviour than material reality (Holstein and Miller, 2006).

Ideas, Global Culture, and Public Discourse Influence Family Life

Other social theorists and researchers believe that focusing on changes in the political economy, social structure, early psychological experiences, or social interaction cannot adequately explain trends in sexuality, relationships, and family life. Instead, they emphasize the importance of ideas and, more recently, of global culture, such as advertising and media representations, when explain-ing personal choices and the creation of lifestyles.

Max Weber (1864–1920), one of the founders of modern sociology, wrote about how prevalent Protestant (especially Calvinist) ideas regarding individ-ualism, hard work, rational conduct, and self-reliance led to the transforma-tion of society and the development of capitalism in the nineteenth century (Abercrombie et al., 1994: 452). Since then, many theorists have focused on the influence of ideas in shaping family life, including the decline in religious authority; the growth of individualism; new ideas about gender equity or body rights; and the desirability of being rich, famous, or changing one's physical appearance through hair dye, piercing, or cosmetic surgery.

Much has been written about the rise of individualism, including the wide-spread and growing belief that people have the right to choose their own marital partners, to be happy in marriage, and to find new partners if their relationships turn out to be unsatisfactory. Particularly the generation born after the Second World War was called the 'me generation' because this cohort placed unprecedented emphasis on their own self-development, education, and personal fulfillment, shunning some of the earlier obligations voiced by their parents. The pre-war generation of women who wanted to further their education and establish careers had been admonished for being selfish and for contributing to the decline of the nuclear family, but the post-war generation was more likely to downplay or disregard these ideas and values.

Post-structuralists have argued that as Western societies grow more consumer-oriented, old expectations and divisions—including the authority of the church and state, social expectations, income differentials, and social class—become less important. Sociologists such as Anthony Giddens (1992), Elisabeth Beck-Gernsheim (2002), and Zygmunt Bauman (2003) have argued that intimacy has been transformed in postmodern society partly by the separation of sex from reproduction but also by the insecurity of relationships and new ideas about 'creating one's own biography'. Freedom from religious and family constraints has encouraged more people to live in ways that differ from their parents, including creating families of choice or groups of close associates with whom they want to spend time rather than spending time with biological relatives who oppose their values and lifestyle.

More people feel that they have the right to create households and lifestyles according to their own beliefs and desires. However, social scientists argue that beliefs and desires are not entirely invented by each individual but rather are shaped by images in the media, advertising, the Internet, films, and global culture. For example, by watching 'extreme makeover' programs on television, we are encouraged to view our wardrobe as 'un-cool', out of fashion, and in need of replacement, and to see our aging bodies as undesirable and in need of expensive repair. We are continually told that our confidence and self-esteem are derived from our personal appearance and sexiness, which encourages us to de-emphasize our personality development, social skills, intellect, occupational accomplishments, and caring responsibilities.

Post-structuralism also 'deconstructs' or questions the origins and intended meanings of certain ideas and beliefs about 'the family', arguing that prevalent images have been socially constructed. As such, they are a product of a certain historical period or organization, and may be used to advance particular political or commercial goals. In the recent past, the family was often conceptualized as a monolithic institution instead of a range of various living patterns that have been transformed over the centuries, that vary by stage throughout the life cycle, and that represent gendered and cultural experiences. In addition, the state uses particular images of family to further its interests. For example, recent discourses surrounding the role of non-custodial parents appeal to moral principles that do not appear to be contentious—that all parents should support their children even after divorce. Yet much of the policy impetus has been driven by more pragmatic financial concerns, such as enforcing private paternal support, as governments committed to dismantling their welfare states redirect responsibility back to families (Mitchell and Goody, 1997; Dalley, 1998).

Public discourse, or the ways that people express certain ideas and the language they use, influences how others see themselves. For example, policy-makers and journalists often talk about 'workless households' or 'welfare moms' when they are discussing mother-led households with incomes assisted by state income support. This discourse encourages the general public to see these mothers in an unflattering light and perhaps to vote for cuts in income support that force beneficiaries into paid work (Mink, 2002). It encourages these mothers to see themselves as social failures who are making no contribution to society even though they may be doing a considerable amount of housework and raising children into healthy and productive adults.

Recent theorizing acknowledges and elaborates differences in family formation and structure, and refutes the 'norm' of the nuclear family, noting that socio-demographic trends in family life in most Western countries are moving in the same direction, as sexuality is becoming separated from marriage, and marriage is being reconstructed as a terminable arrangement with the greater acceptance of serial monogamy. Child-bearing and child-rearing are also becoming separated from marriage, many couples are renegotiating their division of labour, and more same-sex couples are expecting recognition of their living arrangements (Baker, 2006). At the same time, more immigrants with different family patterns are migrating to industrialized countries and indigenous family patterns are being re-acknowledged by governments, social workers, and academics. These social and demographic trends have led to a contestation of the nuclear family as a core concept in both kinship and policy and to a theoretical reworking of what defines family in the twenty-first century.

Methods of Family Research

We have seen that scholars searching for patterns and trends in family life tend to approach their research from a variety of theoretical perspectives, but they also use different methodologies. Most large-scale research projects involve several different methods of investigation at the same time but will always include a thorough review of previous research on the topic. Studies might also use some of the following methods of research: an examination or reanalysis of relevant statistics from official sources; the development of special questionnaires or the reanalysis of older ones; face-to-face interviews; focus groups; personal observations to gain information about the social context; and analysis of historical or policy documents.

Many researchers create their own family-related surveys and send them through the mail or by e-mail, or personally deliver them to participants. For example, a few years ago my research team in New Zealand mailed out a questionnaire to lone mothers who were receiving income support but were still expected to find paid work, asking them to rate their own health and the health of their children, their use of health services, employment-related experiences, and family circumstances. This survey was then compared with a previous study of the wider population. The question behind the **survey research** was whether poor people are more likely to experience poor health, as family health problems are not always considered by policy-makers developing welfare-to-work programs (Baker, 2002a). Some researchers shy away from surveys that ask respondents to choose among specific answers or tick appropriate boxes; they believe that self-answered questionnaires provide superficial data even though answers may come from many participants. Also, the response rates for such surveys are often low (less than 30 per cent).

Family researchers also use personal interviews that include both background contextual questions and open-ended ones where participants can talk at length about their personal circumstances and experiences with a particular family issue. These interviews are often recorded and transcribed in full so they can be analyzed, often with the assistance of computer programs that electronically search for common themes. The New Zealand study mentioned above also involved personal interviews with lone mothers. During these interviews, we investigated the details of family health issues, the mothers' employment experiences, problems with children and former partners, and their views of case management services (Baker and Tippin, 2004). In the same study, we also gained research material from observations in the government office providing case management and income support, from the department's written and electronic advice to their case managers, and from focus groups with the case managers working with lone mothers.

Researchers in most countries must first gain approval from research ethics committees before doing interviews or survey research, to ensure that their projects have the informed consent of participants, do no harm, respect people's privacy, and keep their answers confidential and anonymous. Ethics committees, comprised of researchers and community members, are particularly vigilant when researchers want to talk to 'vulnerable subjects', such as children, beneficiaries, or abused women. Family researchers do not need ethics approval if they rely only on the analysis of public policy documents, personal diaries, family law reforms, court records, or documents from government departments, although they certainly need the approval of the departments involved.

Researchers may also reanalyze official statistics, using the government census, labour market statistics, or household surveys to uncover changes such as trends in maternal employment or rates of cohabitation, marriage, fertility, and divorce. However, official statistics are not available on all topics within family studies and these statistics usually provide less information than specialized studies, especially those that talk at length to people in their own homes. Yet meeting ethics requirements, finding people who are willing to participate in research projects, talking to individuals in their homes, and mailing out surveys can be challenging and costly in terms of both time and money. Researchers often have quite different opinions about which method of research is the best for their particular family project. They are sometimes asked to research a topic in a certain way by a government department or other research sponsor. Therefore, the method of research used in family studies, as in other subject areas, might be influenced by a number of factors, including ideas about the validity and wisdom of certain methods of research, the time and resources available for research, requirements of the sponsors, or the availability of existing data. In fact, practical constraints may outweigh academic ones when researchers decide which method to use in their search for new knowledge about family life.

Conclusion

Over the past two decades, academics have re-conceptualized the study of families. They now place more emphasis on identity formation, gendered and cultural experiences, influences from global culture on family life, balancing caring and earning, and the analysis of political discourse. The growth of post-structural theorizing in the social sciences and humanities has influenced much of research and theory on family, sexuality, and gender, as more academics now acknowledge the considerable diversity in household formation, lifestyles, and identities that vary in different social settings, throughout the life course and throughout history. Although some academics adhere to one theoretical or methodological approach and view all others as mutually exclusive, most combine several approaches or borrow ideas from more than one perspective.

Many scholars now argue that family life in advanced industrial societies has become more fragmented and complex with a number of sources of differentiation, including social class, gender, sexual preference, ethnicity, and age (Abercrombie et al., 1994: 326). Furthermore, social conditions are dominated by economic markets that are internationally competitive, specialized, and non-unionized. Popular culture has become more consumer-oriented and more young people and families are falling into debt. At the same time, some governments have been attempting to dismantle aspects of the welfare state, arguing that families need to be more self-sufficient and less dependent on state income support.

These issues are acknowledged within the theoretical framework of this book, which gives priority to a **feminist political economy perspective** but also draws on post-structural research. By this I mean that analysis of gender relations is central to this book, but I also focus on the ways that family income, education, laws, and cultural practices influence people's intimate relationships and personal desires. At the same time, I note the areas where choices can be made (and are actually made) to create people's own biographies.

In the next chapter, I discuss social research relating to relationship formation, which includes how people find sexual partners, who they select as 'dates' and 'mates', and at what stage in their lives they seek permanent intimate relationships. The two basic questions we ask are which patterns are new and how do we explain the changes?

Summary

The chapter concludes that the academic and policy definitions of family need to be sufficiently broad to encompass the variations in structure and experience, as 'family' is conceptualized differently in other cultures, in various theoretical frameworks, and by different government departments. The chapter also concludes that choice of theoretical framework shapes the focus of family investigations, the findings of research, and how findings are interpreted.

Questions for Critical Thought

1. Is there any evidence that expectations about family life and actual family patterns are becoming more similar around the world with urbanization, international travel, and Internet usage?

2. Can we understand anything useful about family life by studying political discourse, or the portrayal of family life in television serials and women's magazines?

3. Which research method provides more useful information about family life: an email survey or face-to-face interviews?

Suggested Readings

Giddens, Anthony. 2006. *Sociology*, 5th edn. Cambridge: Polity Press. Chapter 4 of this British textbook contains a good summary of general sociological theories, and Chapter 7 discusses family theories.

Luxton, Meg. 2009. 'Conceptualizing "Families": Theoretical Frameworks', in M. Baker, ed., *Families: Changing Trends in Canada*, 6th edn. Toronto: McGraw-Hill Ryerson, 29–51. This chapter discusses three major sociological theories about the nature of family life.

Poole, Marilyn, ed. 2004. *Family: Changing Families, Changing Times.* Melbourne: Allen & Unwin. This text explores contemporary Australian family life.

Suggested Websites ───────────────────

Australian Institute of Family Studies *www.aifs.gov.au*
This website provides numerous statistics and research papers on family life in Australia.

Vanier Institute of the Family, Canada *www.vifamily.ca*
This privately funded organization based in Ottawa provides educational material, news items, and research on Canadian families. The Vanier Institute also publishes a magazine called *Transition*.

Families Commission, New Zealand *www.nzfamilies.org.nz*
This government-funded agency produces many online research reports including New Zealand and international information on families.

Chapter 2

Forming Relationships

Learning Objectives

- To relate patterns in dating and sexual behaviour to the changing social context over the decades
- To differentiate between social attitudes and actual behaviour relating to sexuality
- To search for social patterns in marital choices

Chapter Outline

This chapter discusses some aspects of the social history of dating and courtship in order to understand why young people were pressured to choose a 'suitable' partner and marry according to their social position and family preferences. The chapter also examines current dating practices and partnering choices, both inside and outside of marriage.

Introduction

Do men and women still search for similar kinds of intimate partners or do they locate partners and develop relationships differently from a **generation** or two ago? Family researchers continue to search for new trends in dating and family formation because these can provide insights into wider social change. In this chapter we note that ways of locating new partners and establishing relationships have changed somewhat over the years in most Western countries. Essentially, developing intimate partnerships has become easier, less formalized, less gendered, and more a matter of personal choice.

Nevertheless, traditional attitudes and practices remain and some of the same gendered and cultural patterns underpin personal preferences. Furthermore, current research suggests that the timing of first sexual experiences and partner choices continues to be shaped by family circumstances, social pressures from 'significant others', social class background, and cultural expectations.

The state of the economy and opportunities for education and work can also influence the timing of family formation, whether or not couples become parents, and the number of children they actually have compared to the number they desire.

In Western industrialized countries, most people choose their own intimate partners, although elders in some cultural communities try to assist their young people to form viable partnerships and to prevent unsuitable liaisons. Among cultural groups that encourage arranged or partially **arranged marriage**, dating is seldom tolerated because parents expect to control their children's heterosexual relationships and the timing of their marriages. Potential partners are identified by elders from kin networks or from the cultural community and the young people involved do not always know each other in advance. Supervised meetings between the potential partners and negotiations between the two families determine whether or not a marriage will take place, but young people now have more say in marriage decisions, including the opportunity to veto some or all of their parents' choices. The laws of all westernized countries support free-choice marriages by requiring the written consent of both the bride and the groom. This means that, at least theoretically, no one living in these countries can be coerced into a wedding, even within cultural communities practising arranged marriages.

In free-choice relationships, individuals may spend several years attending social functions or enjoying leisure activities with several different intimate or sexual partners before making any concrete plans to cohabit or share the future with any of them. Eventually, however, most individuals develop an exclusive relationship that they would like to be ongoing or permanent. Nowadays, many people cohabit in a marriage-like relationship before making a long-term commitment, a pattern that used to be unacceptable, especially in middle- and upper-class society. Choosing a partner is usually based on such factors as physical attraction, similar outlooks and interests, compatible personalities, desire for emotional stability and parenthood, and love. However, these characteristics may depend on the type of relationship wanted at the time. Distinctions normally are made among the attributes expected from a 'one-night stand', a suitable dating partner, a compatible cohabitation partner, and one who is potentially 'marriageable' for life. What patterns are apparent in the way individuals make these decisions?

Dating as a Recent Social Phenomenon

Social history and comparative family studies reveal that current dating practices are relatively recent in westernized countries and are not as widespread as we might think in other parts of the world. The origins of romantic love in Europe date back to feudal times (Schultz, 2006). Marriages at that time were arranged—to suit family alliances, to provide heirs, and to improve or maintain family wealth—and 'love' was not considered essential to the participants in the contract. Husbands and wives were not expected to have their emotional needs satisfied in marriage, although that sometimes did happen. Instead, they sought satisfaction in their children, their work, in same-sex friendships, or in other relationships.

People of the higher classes were more likely to develop love relationships but these were often outside marriage and did not always involve sexual activity. Instead, they involved idealized (romanticized) love, public acts of gallantry, and deferential attention. Acts of chivalry, or treating noblewomen with extra respect, accorded a new kind of power to women beyond their roles as wives and chatelaines and their potential capacity to produce heirs to their estates. Women, in the courtly love relationship, were recognized as holding the power to subdue the male through innocent affection. This, along with related attitudes developed through greater honour accorded to the Virgin Mary in the Christian church, helped to dissociate wealthy women from material interests. That is, the woman became less a chattel and overseer of domestic staff and property, and more a personal influence in the male sphere. Noblewomen exerted their influence by virtue of inherited position and wealth, as well as personal abilities. Of course, women of other classes, like their male peers, were more nearly slaves or chattels, with the exception of those who earned status within the church or through businesses of some sort.

From the eighteenth century, with the rise of a wealthy middle class, social power began to shift from the nobility to those who possessed economic strength. The gradual depletion of power from the aristocracy (sometimes very dramatically through revolution, as in France and the United States) granted political powers to a new class of bourgeois males through voting. Not all men, however, were immediately enfranchised; property and wealth continued to determine a man's right to vote, even though men became politically influential on a much broader scale. During the eighteenth and nineteenth centuries, partly through increasing opportunities for education, many more women moved from the impoverished to the middle classes but they had difficulty matching the status of their male partners. Women's sphere of influence remained much more domestic. Furthermore, until the late nineteenth and early twentieth centuries, women were not allowed to take political office, own land, or work in business or the professions, and rich women had servants to do the housework. Men's 'chivalrous' behaviour towards women became formalized and perhaps a form of compensation—a way of keeping women happy despite their relatively low economic and legal status (Leslie and Korman, 1989: 173). As society became politically more egalitarian, some of these chivalrous customs disappeared while others remained as etiquette—such as men opening doors for women, helping them on with their coats, or protecting them from rain or heavy work.

The vast majority of people in Europe and in the colonies were poor and lived in crowded and unsanitary conditions that did not permit much romance or chivalry. Survival usually meant long hours of work. Most unmarried adults lived with their parents and siblings, and were not encouraged to spend time alone with eligible partners. Although people made choices based on love as well as on economic or other factors, the leisure and privacy required to maintain romance after the wedding were difficult to find (Skolnick, 1987). Married couples shared their small living spaces with their children, who sometimes arrived within a year of the wedding, and couples occasionally shared accommodation with other relatives or boarders. Consequently, household members would not be able to disguise their sexual activity, their bodily functions, their illnesses, or other aspects of personal life from others. Nevertheless, most young people anticipated marriage and parenthood because they were synonymous with adulthood, maturity, respectability, and authority within the community. They also anticipated the sexual relationship, but that was socially approved only within matrimony. Economics played a large role in the pairing process, however; in poorer families, parents wanted their sons and daughters to marry wealthier persons who would help them out of debt and bring productive land into the family. They wanted a child to marry a partner who was kind but who was also an industrious, strong, and healthy person who would bring grandchildren to the family and who would be able to care for them in their declining years.

Even before marriages were based on love, many children probably persuaded their parents to arrange a marriage with people they already knew and wanted to marry. Many married partners grew to love each other deeply after sharing their lives, even when their marriage was partially arranged. Despite the fact that the male head of the household had considerable authority over other family members, there were undoubtedly fathers and husbands who were sensitive to the wishes of their wives and children. Ideal family systems in the past differed considerably from reality, as they still do today. Even when chastity before marriage was considered an essential virtue, many young men frequented prostitutes or had secret sexual liaisons. Married men and, less often, married women had secret affairs, but without reliable contraception, premarital pregnancies were disguised with hasty marriages, adoptions, or backstreet abortions and extramarital pregnancies were passed off as children of the existing marriage or terminated with an illegal abortion.

In the first half of the twentieth century, most unmarried young people in both urban and rural areas continued to live with their parents or relatives, and few adolescents or young adults lived with peers before marriage (Nett, 1993: 216). While living with family, most young people paid 'room and board' and engaged in unpaid chores to help cover household expenses. If they lived apart from their parents to attend school or earn money, they usually boarded with relatives or lived in supervised residences or boarding houses with little privacy.

Working long hours without much leisure time meant that young people had few opportunities to party, to date widely, or to develop more than one intimate relationship before they married for life (Bradbury, 2005). Furthermore, social rules reinforced by the church permitted men and women little opportunity to spend time alone together in public or in private, unless they were engaged or married. Those who lived in remote areas would also have had few opportunities to meet suitable partners.

Securing a marriage partner was essential for young women partly because they were excluded from most employment and were less likely to inherit the family farm or business. Even if they found wage work, women earned considerably less than men and most employed women were unable to fully support themselves and/or their children. Generally, the woman needed a husband to earn sufficient money to run the household, to perform heavy chores around the house, to 'cherish' her, and to provide her with children (who raised her status within the family and community). Similarly, few men could survive without a wife to cook, clean the home, launder the clothes, grow vegetables, provide him with sexual satisfaction, and raise the children. Housework was very time-consuming and laborious before electricity, refrigeration, and imported food. Wage labourers normally worked long hours each weekday as well as Saturday mornings, and farmers worked every day. Before the 1930s, few employees were entitled to paid holidays. The banks and food stores were closed by the time most men finished work, leaving little opportunity to run personal errands after work. Wealthy men could afford live-in servants, but most needed a wife to manage the household.

Young people met their potential spouses at school, in their neighbourhood, at their church, or through their siblings and other relatives. Sometimes they were introduced by friends or family members, and occasionally they were 'set up' by friends on 'blind dates'. They also met partners at dances, parties, and other social functions, but these were usually community activities attended by a variety of age groups, where the activities of young people were closely monitored by adult chaperones to ensure that no 'unseemly conduct' occurred. These activities were based on expectations of heterosexuality, as intimate relationships among same-sex couples were either illegal or not condoned.

The Social Regulation of Courtship

In nineteenth-century North America, as well as in other liberal welfare states, courtship, love, and marriage were constrained by an intricate network of social, institutional, and familial influences (Shorter, 1975; Ward, 1990). From the eighteenth century, young men increasingly took the initiative to find their own brides but were expected to ask the father's permission to 'court' her, or gradually develop a relationship leading to marriage. This sometimes involved a formal meeting, at which the young man addressed the woman's father formally and presented his credentials, somewhat like a job interview. The father, as well as other relatives, wanted to ensure that the suitor's intentions were 'honourable', which meant that he sincerely intended to marry the daughter rather than just wanted a 'good time' that would ruin her reputation. The father also expected some assurance that the intended fiancé would become a kind, thoughtful, and faithful husband who could adequately support his daughter. The father's permission might be acquired either before the 'courtship' began or before any formal marriage proposal was accepted by the woman (Ward, 1990).

Women were expected to encourage only one or two such courtships before marriage. When the man's proposal was accepted, the engagement (or betrothal) was publicly announced and thus became a binding agreement. However, the wedding might be delayed until the male partner more firmly established his work life or career, until he saved money, or until he was able to persuade his employer to raise his earnings or his father to share farm earnings or even to hand over the farm. The 'banns'—the couple's intentions to marry—were then read in church for three consecutive Sundays to ensure that anyone who knew of a reason why the marriage should not take place would have the opportunity to speak out. This was largely to ensure against 'bigamy' or marriage to more than one partner at a time. Later, when the state became more involved in legalizing marriage, a licence was also required to ensure that marriage partners were acceptable and appropriate from the viewpoint of community leaders and the government. However, most weddings continued to be held in places of worship until the 1960s or later.

Most young people did not develop relationships with a variety of potential partners before marriage because once a man and woman were seen together several times they became viewed by friends and relatives as a 'couple'. However, many young people voluntarily committed themselves to their teenage sweetheart through lengthy formal engagements, which then meant that no other dating partners could be accepted without violating the unspoken agreement of exclusivity. Marriage was important to the social and economic well-being of both men and women. Young women, especially, attempted to secure a partner before they became older than their marrying peers ('left on the shelf' without a partner) or found their cohort of suitable partners shrinking so that they felt forced to marry someone less desirable. Marital choices were often limited to neighbours, school or work acquaintances, and family friends because most young people attended local schools, entered the workforce at a young age, or cared for their elderly parents at home, but did not travel outside their community unless they were financially well off.

Box 2.1 Courtship and Rural Dances in New Zealand, 1880s to 1920s

Courtship was an expected and important aspect of rural dances. The process of courtship was not simply about romance and love, however. Choosing a partner involved choosing a way of life, and single people had certain expectations of their prospective partners. Men wanted wives who had the ability to manage a home economically under difficult circumstances. Women looked for traits such as the ability to run a farm smoothly...

The ways people dressed and presented themselves at the local dance were also linked to notions of courtship and romance. Particularly for young women, the ritual of 'coming out'—of being a debutante at a local dance—symbolised their progression to womanhood and their ability to accept offers of romance....The hours of preparation which women put into their costumes were related to perceptions of wealth and domestic ability....In re-making dresses, women were expressing values of thrift and productivity. Their dress demonstrated their usefulness as wives as well as their marital availability...

The dance provided rural people with important and necessary opportunities for courtship and romance. For courting couples, the dance was an opportunity to display their status as a couple, and also to progress through their courtship under community supervision. For the unattached, it was the venue to find a suitable partner. Family and neighbours encouraged romance at dances, and courtship at social occasions was seen as a necessary and important aspect of community life. In a society in which marriage was an expectation, the dance provided the ideal environment in which to pursue romance. Furthermore, the social occasion gave young women the opportunity to enter the arena of courtship and display the material possessions and dress that symbolised their progression to womanhood. The dance, like the ball-gown, was a multi-layered affair: fundamentally a means of entertainment, but with many hidden meanings, purposes and outcomes.

Source: Excerpts from Emma Dewson. 2004. 'Off to the Dance: Romance in Rural New Zealand Communities, 1880s–1920s', *History Australia* 2: 1 (December).

According to public norms, sexuality was supposed to be restricted to marriage or at least to heterosexual couples who were formally engaged, although, clearly, a **double standard** existed for men and women. Premarital chastity was deemed more important for women, and those who proceeded to sexual intercourse were expected to marry quickly. If they did not, they could be perceived by other men as fair game for sexual advances or harassment. These women would be seen by other parents as 'damaged goods' or 'having a past', a reputation that would reduce their future chances of finding a suitable partner. However, men could use commitment, expressions of love, or formal engagement to gain sexual favours from their girlfriends, and women could use the expectation of premarital chastity to pressure their boyfriends into a marriage proposal and formal engagement. If pregnancy occurred before marriage, their families and friends would pressure them to cement their relationship in legal marriage and to stay together for life. Consequently, some couples married hastily but were expected to live with the consequences.

Before the 1940s, middle-class parents seldom permitted their daughters to participate in leisure activities involving young men without the presence of chaperones, who might have been other relatives, servants, reliable neighbours, school teachers, or clergy. This was particularly the case for wealthier families, who valued female premarital chastity more than poorer families did. Rich families had more to lose in terms of lost reputation or family wealth if their daughters were forced into hasty ('shotgun') weddings with 'inappropriate' partners. Some wealthy parents engaged companions to travel with their unmarried daughters in order to protect their reputations, but many middle-class parents simply restricted their daughters' activities outside the household. If there was any suspicion of sexual misconduct, and this was very broadly defined, a woman's chances of making a 'good marriage' would be reduced.

For middle-class women, a good marriage meant one to a kind, considerate man from the same religious and ethnic group who worked hard and earned a steady income that was high enough to support a wife and several children. He was also expected to come from a similar social class, preferably from a reputable family known by the woman's parents, relatives, or neighbours. A good marriage was also a gendered one, with **complementary roles** for husband and wife, who were said to be separate but equal. For middle-class men, a suitable marriage meant one to an attractive, respectable woman with social skills, a pleasant personality, good health and child-bearing potential, and valuable skills in homemaking and money management. Education was desirable but middle-class women were expected to become homemakers and mothers after marriage rather than wage earners. A good wife also behaved in a respectable and socially appropriate manner. If she did not, she could damage her husband's career prospects, his personal reputation, and their shared social life.

Early in the twentieth century, only men were expected to propose marriage. Young men hesitated to propose or to finalize marriage arrangements until they could afford to support a wife and children because men were automatically designated as the family earner when they married. Engaged women who had paid jobs were expected to leave their employment as their wedding date approached, regardless of how interesting or lucrative their jobs were. They were expected to prepare for their wedding day and their marriage, when they would be responsible for ensuring that the home was a pleasant place and that the domestic chores were done.

Before the 1960s, the amount of housework was greater and more time-consuming than today. Physical means of birth control were also unreliable and socially unacceptable, with babies expected shortly after marriage. Reticence, sublimation of sexuality through work, and sexual self-control were widely practised as means of limiting the number of pregnancies for a couple. Couples had to save sufficient resources and the man had to acquire a steady income before they could afford to marry and establish a household separate from their parents. Without social security programs or credit cards, men often had to ask their employers for higher wages or ask their parents for a loan in order to manage their new commitments. If the boss or parents agreed, the couple could marry, but many had to postpone their marriage plans for financial reasons. In some cases, parents or other relatives also objected to the match or pressed the couple to postpone the wedding until the man completed his education or the couple saved more money.

The Great Depression of the 1930s forced many couples to delay marriage and also made people conscious of material security in a number of ways, encouraging them to focus on thrift, hard work, and self-sufficiency. In those days, few state income support programs or subsidized health-care services were available, especially in the liberal welfare states, and families needed to save money for accommodation, food, clothing, transportation, and future health-care costs, which included doctor's fees for normal childbirths but also for childbirth complications or accidents. Credit cards were not widely used until the 1970s and any credit given was at the personal discretion of the shopkeeper or the doctor.

Until the 1950s, rules of **endogamy** were also quite strict. For example, dating and engagements between Protestants and Catholics were frowned upon in many countries, but public opinion especially opposed interracial, intercultural, and interfaith liaisons. Most people attended regular religious services and their church leaders encouraged high moral values and family behaviour that was gendered, endogamous, and favoured reproduction. In addition, parents and schoolteachers attempted to maintain strict authority over the behaviour of children and young people. Although some children from large, poor, and rural families spent more time out of the view of their parents and teachers than they might today, young people were generally given fewer choices about any aspect of their lives, with rigid and hierarchical social rules of behaviour at home, school, work, and in the community.

The Second World War became a turning point for many social attitudes and behavioural patterns, including dating and sexual practices. Dating, premarital sex, and abortion rates increased sharply during the war when young people were away from parents and chaperones (Kedgley, 1996: 148; Baker, 2001b). When soldiers were on leave at home or in foreign countries, they tended to take more risks with their sexual partners, as life seemed so dangerous and short and pleasures were few. Many couples married hastily before or during the war, which enabled them to live together when the man was on leave and to have sex without social disapproval. Wartime marriages also increased the social and economic security of the brides and gave the grooms some hope of future domestic security when they returned home (if they survived combat). However, rates of separation, annulments, and divorces increased when men returned home from the war. Many relationships did not survive the long separation, which sometimes lasted for years when men were posted overseas or taken prisoner. Couples drifted apart, either the man or the woman met a new partner, and some wives could not cope with their husbands' wartime injuries, especially when they were psychological (Montgomerie, 1999).

By the late 1940s, dating without chaperones had become widespread, but this was replaced by strictly gendered etiquette rules. For example, men were permitted to invite women to attend social functions with them but women were not allowed to ask men, at least not directly. Men were expected to provide the transportation and pay for all the expenses, while women were urged to behave as congenial, attractive, and accommodating companions. Post-war affluence gave middle-class individuals more choice in clothing, food, and entertainments; couples continued to 'dress up' for dating (depending on the venue). They attended social events such as dances or films, or they simply went for a walk in a public park or down the main street of town. As late as the 1930s, middle-class men might have dressed in a hat, jacket, and tie, and women in a dress, high-heeled shoes, hat, and gloves simply in order to go for a walk together in a public park and then return to one of their family homes for dinner.

Before the 1950s, people differentiated between 'dating' and 'courtship'. Dating was defined as a short period of getting acquainted with the available partners, while courtship involved developing a serious relationship with one partner leading to lifelong marriage. Men were given the freedom to date more widely than women and were generally accorded a wider social range. A woman who invited frequent dates (flirted) and made herself to some degree sexually available to them all without distinction would be considered 'fast' or 'loose', which damaged her reputation and future chances of a good marriage. Dating activities were usually relatively public and were not supposed to include solitary or intimate activities other than hand-holding or chaste good-night kisses. Couple activities particularly excluded any expectation of sexual intercourse, although we know that many unmarried couples did engage in sexual activities from records of illegal abortions, illegitimate births, adoptions, hasty marriages, and 'premature' babies.

The move from dating to courtship usually involved the man proposing marriage to the woman. If she agreed, he often bought her an engagement ring made of gold or silver with a precious stone such as a diamond to represent high value and durability. This engagement ring symbolized their lifelong commitment and became a public contractual agreement to marry that could not be easily broken without mutual consent. If an engaged woman broke off the engagement, she was expected to return the ring. If he backed out after she or her family had made costly wedding preparations, she could sue him for 'breach of promise' under English common law and possibly receive a payment for 'damages' at the jury's discretion (Ward, 1990: 32). However, few jilted fiancées had the money to engage a lawyer and many knew that their former fiancé could not afford to pay even if they were successful in a civil lawsuit.

When men and women became engaged, their friends and family would allow them more privacy and intimate relations. However, if she became pregnant, parents and friends would have pressured the couple to marry quickly before the pregnancy was noticed by others. Ideas about social propriety were almost more important than the couple's feelings for each other or their future chances of marital happiness. As a result, many couples were pressured into marriage prematurely by unintended pregnancy. If an unmarried pregnant woman was unable or unwilling to marry or to have an (illegal) abortion, she might leave her community to give birth, surrender the infant for adoption (agencies insisted on a two-parent family for adoption), and return quietly to the community. Private or church-run maternity homes assisted many unmarried mothers through childbirth and arranged for the adoption of their children. Otherwise, these women would have been subjected to disapproval or ostracism, and would have brought disrepute to themselves and their families. Early in the twentieth century, 'closed adoption' practices were widespread, which sometimes meant that birth certificates were altered and no further contact was permitted between birth mothers and their infants.

If conception occurred before the wedding date, engaged couples might simply bring forward the marriage ceremony rather than permit the child to be adopted or to be (illegally) aborted. Their earlier wedding date would ensure that the child was 'legitimate'. A legitimate child was born with a legal father and was permitted to take his surname and inherit from him, whereas an illegitimate child took the mother's surname, had no legal rights from the father, and was stigmatized socially as a 'bastard'.

This brief overview of past practices suggests that people had limited choices about sexuality and relationships because strict rules of behaviour were enforced within families, communities, and workplaces, as well as internalized. Even when individuals or couples disagreed with the rules or with their parents' wishes, few could afford, either financially or socially, to contravene them.

Current Dating and Sexual Practices

Since the 1960s, young people have gradually moved away from rigid and gendered expectations of dating and 'courting' (Crouter and Booth, 2006; Sweeney, 2006). More people now attend social activities as individuals or groups rather than as couples, and others arrange to meet potential partners at social events. Improvements in contraception since the 1960s have enabled premarital sex without pregnancy, which has liberalized both attitudes and behaviours. In addition, sexuality has become a marketable commodity that is romanticized in the media and sold in the consumer-oriented economy as fantasies and pleasures (McDaniel and Tepperman, 2000: 132).

British sociologist Anthony Giddens (1992) described the new sexuality as 'plastic' because it was something to be discovered, moulded, and altered. However, other researchers have argued that the double standard of sexuality (with men having more freedom) has been eroded but it has not entirely disappeared. Women have become more assertive in dating practices but Mongeau and Carey (1996) found that American men are more likely than women to interpret a first date initiated by a woman as a sexual overture. Coltrane (1998) found that men see 'sexually aggressive women' as off-putting, although flirting with sexual overtones is still an integral part of dating for both men and women. Research has also confirmed that parents monitor their daughter's dating activities more closely than their son's, such as establishing stricter behavioural expectations, prescriptions, and rules (Madsen, 2008).

Bogle (2008) found that many college-aged young adults in the United States arrive at social events alone or in groups but 'hook up' with partners for casual sex or the potential development of longer-term relationships. After a relationship has been established, an urban couple might attend a film or concert together or go to a bar or café, where they might share the expenses or the better-off of the two might pay, and then they might end up at one or the other's apartment or flat to listen to music, watch a video, talk, and/or make love. However, the unclear rules of the 'hook up script' leave young women 'to learn the hard way' to have low expectations of forming a relationship and that the double standard of sexual behaviour still applies (ibid.). Bogle found that students generally believed that others 'went further' or hooked up more often than they did. Furthermore, peer pressure and female competition for scarce relationships favour men's desire for multiple partners and casual encounters. Women felt pressured to 'dress up' for men and to try to impress them, but were labelled as 'easy' or 'dirty' if they had 'too many' partners. She also found that exclusive couple relationships can develop from hooking up but it is men who typically decide to evolve the relationship. Once these American students graduate from university, Bogle found that their dating expectations become more traditional, with more women expecting men to ask them out, pick them up for dates, and pay the expenses (Walsh, 2008).

Other research has also found that heterosexual women spend a considerable amount of time and money making themselves attractive to men and gendered patterns still exist in ideal partners (Abu-Laban and McDaniel, 1998; Crouter and Booth, 2006). Introduction services and dating agencies rely on some of the same characteristics found to be important when people seek their own partners, including similar cultural, religious, and educational backgrounds—but with the man older, more educated, and taller. Introduction services also show videos to their clients of potential partners, acknowledging that many choices are based on physical appearance, first impressions, or 'chemistry'. In a recent experimental study of speed dating in the United States, women's decisions emphasized men's intelligence, race, and affluence while men responded more to women's physical attractiveness, devaluing women's intelligence and ambition if it seemed greater than theirs (Fisman et al., 2006).

Desired characteristics in a dating partner still emphasize women's youthful appearance and men's height, strength, and occupational success (McDaniel and Tepperman, 2004; Bogle, 2008). According to **exchange theory**, the closer the body approximates idealized images of youth and beauty, the higher its 'exchange value', especially for women's bodies (Featherstone, 1991). Structural theorists argue that men's preferences for younger, attractive women and women's preference for taller, successful, older men can lead to a 'marriage squeeze'. This means that people edged out of the **marriage market** are older and less conventionally attractive women, and younger and shorter men with low education and incomes. Although men continue to search for younger women who are slim and attractive, research also suggests that women's earning capacity is becoming more important for 'assortative mating', at least to white American men (Sweeney, 2004).

A study by Chilla Bulbeck (cited in Connolly, 2004) revealed that Australian teenagers have retained gendered expectations about future partners. The researchers asked secondary school students from South Australia and Western Australia to imagine their future at age 70 and 80 and to reflect on the successes and failures in their lives. Despite three decades of discussion about gender equity, teenage boys wrote about a future of wealth, sex with many beautiful women, fast cars, and sport. Although 65 per cent of the girls said that they wanted a career, their stories focused on romance, meeting Mr Right, shared parenting, and relationships involving mutual understanding. A man's earning capacity is still relevant to some girls, and being rich and famous was highlighted by many of the boys. The author noted that the expectations of future fame and wealth are quite unrealistic, but also that discrepancies

Box 2.2 Australian Young Women* and Their Imagined Futures

'The preparations for the wedding took up most of my time when I wasn't at work...It was one of the best moments of my life. I had a beautiful wedding dress, nice flowers and all of my family was there from Adelaide. We went to Venice for our honeymoon, it was the one place I hadn't been.' (Female, middle-class government girls' school)

'I do plan on having a 'happening' social life. This life involves dancing, drinking and promiscuity (I will only be promiscuous once I've fallen in love, had my heart broken and vowed to never fall in love again). Don't worry, I'll be safe, go on the pill so I won't fall pregnant...I want to have an apartment/house at the beach and I want to own tropical fish. I would also like to own the Lackleys Cinema and still charge $7.50 for a double feature. And I would like to meet Paul Newman.' (Female, Catholic girls' school)

* in their final year of high school.

Source: Chilla Bulbeck. 2005. '"Women are Exploited Way Too Often", Feminist Rhetorics at the End of Equality', *Australian Feminist Studies* 20, 46 (March): 71–2.

between the stories of men and women encouraged her to predict more divorce in the future (ibid.).

Sociologists now talk about 'commodity feminism' or 'postfeminism' in which young women claim to gain 'girl power' by taking on traditionally male jobs or becoming celebrities, while dressing in an openly sexual way with all of the trappings of traditional femininity (such as lacy undergarments, dark lipstick, dyed hair, sequins, and high-heeled shoes) (Hopkins, 2002; Bulbeck, 2005). Poststructural feminists argue that these women 'choose to do femininity' in their own innovative way rather than rejecting it as liberal feminists seemed to do in the 1970s. However, this 'choice' is so often focused on consumerism and overt sexuality, which could encourage other people to perceive and treat these women as sexual 'objects' rather than as competent and intelligent human beings.

Imagined partners are sexually/physically attractive and successful, but we also expect them to be considerate of our feelings and to share similar values and interests. Although some people dismiss or flaunt prevalent expectations, researchers continue to find that most people still internalize the importance of choosing a partner from a similar social background or from the gendered hierarchy in social and physical characteristics. Furthermore, parents still worry that their children will short-change themselves by choosing a partner who is 'not good enough' for them.

Despite general insistence on the importance of personal choice in locating dating and marriage partners, high rates of separation and divorce among couples suggest that decisions may not be based on qualities that lead to lasting relationships. Personal judgments based on physical appearance and sexuality are widespread in the popular media. Relationship instability is actually being encouraged by focusing on sexuality, fashionable appearance, and material success rather than shared values, companionship, or knowledge of the person's personality or background. Heavy reliance on appearance contributes to short-term relationships in cultures that already focus on individualism, self-development, and personal choice.

Dating Abuse

Much of the research on dating violence and **abuse** has been done in North America. One of the first studies was conducted among American university students by Makepeace (1981), who reported that one in five dating relationships contained some elements of physical **violence**. During the 1990s, the Canadian government invested research money on this topic and Barnes, Greenwood, and Sommers (1991) found that 42 per cent of Canadian dating relationships among students in tertiary institutions included violence. DeKeseredy and Schwartz (1994) also found that Canadian girls who experience violence in elementary school are more likely to become victims of dating violence in college and university.

More recent American and Canadian studies link childhood experiences of maltreatment, parental conflict, and domestic violence with more involvement with adolescent dating violence, both as perpetrators and victims (Tschann et al., 2009; Wolfe et al., 2009). This research clearly indicates that abuse and violence is not confined to marital relationships. Research has also found that some young women who are abused remain with their abusive boyfriends, even misperceiving the abuse as an indication of love.

External factors such as economic dependency and presence of children contribute to wives' decisions to remain with abusive partners but these factors are rarely present in dating relationships. Some researchers explain the willingness to remain in an abusive dating relationship by the pervasiveness of abuse in heterosexual relationships but also by arguing that some young people are socialized to view gender relations as a 'battle of the sexes'. Women who stay in an abusive dating relationship may have lower self-esteem, feelings of obligation to the abuser, fear of reprisal, or have experienced an upbringing that normalized physical, sexual, or verbal abuse.

Finding Partners: Advertising versus Tradition

For decades, people have been advertising in newspapers for intimate partners. In 1982, I analyzed personal advertisements in a Canadian daily newspaper, including the ways that heterosexual men and women described themselves and what they asked for in potential partners (Baker, 1982). Men and women tended to present themselves in traditional gendered ways despite this apparently unconventional way of seeking a partner. Men more often described themselves as 'tall' and 'successful' business or professional men, gave their age, and asked for 'attractive' younger women for a lasting relationship or 'recreational sex'. In contrast, women tended to describe themselves as petite, slim, and attractive and asked for business or professional men who were the same age or older. Just as in previous decades, women focused on lasting relationships or marriage. Similar gendered advertisements were found in Canadian newspapers from 1975 to 1988 by Sev'er (1990).

In a content analysis of 1,094 personal advertisements from four British newspapers, Jagger (2005) found that 61 per cent of advertisers were men but more of the advertisers over 45 years old were women. Men were more likely to mention their age but more women qualified their age in some way that suggested it was problematic. For example, they described themselves as 'a very young 39-year-old female', '55 years young', or 'young 60-year-old widow'; or they described themselves in the language of 'positive aging', providing an optimistic, upbeat, physically active version of self. Jagger also noted the relative youthfulness of the advertisers using qualifying statements about age, with both males and females in their thirties revealing age-conscious identities ('male 37 but feels much younger'). The devaluation of age and aging has implications for advertisers when marketing the self, and advertisers seem to feel the need to reconcile the way they look with the way they feel (Turner, 1995; Jagger, 2005).

In Jagger's study, most people who stated an age preference wanted someone of a comparable age to themselves but men were more likely than women to ask for a younger partner. Among the older advertisers, men were most likely to say that they wanted a younger or much younger woman, although nearly one-fifth of older women also requested a younger man. Jagger (2005) showed that the ability to negotiate lifestyle choices from a diversity of options is shaped in complex ways by gender and age, but argued that individuals are still negotiating their identities around socially proscribed expectations that focus on the value of youth.

When people advertised for 'companions' in the newspaper, they often spoke on the telephone before meeting in person, and then first met in a public place for their personal safety. Now, more people search for partners on the Internet where they can screen candidates with preliminary questions about their habits and interests and provide detailed self-descriptions before agreeing to talk on the telephone or meet in person. However, creating a false identity either in newspaper advertising or on the Internet is easy, and it can be particularly dangerous to assume that you know someone through e-mail correspondence when you actually have never met the person or even spoken to them.

The Internet is now used to form relationships and arrange to meet for sex. Internet relationships transcend geographical distance and are forged on the basis of common interests rather than on common locality. They are disembodied, which provides more scope for fantasy, deception, and experimentation, making it possible to explore identities and sexualities. Men can pretend to be women and women can pretend to be men. Finally, these relationships tend to be uninhibited, which means that people can engage in more self-disclosure and riskier or harmful behaviour (Gilding, 2002). Relationships formed through cyberspace have been called 'hyperpersonal' because some people can reveal more of themselves, feel more attraction, and express more emotions on a keyboard than face-to-face. Instead of worrying about their looks, they can concentrate on the message (Wallace, 1999).

Research on Internet dating has demonstrated that people can be rather strategic in the way they present themselves in cyberspace (Whitty, 2007). One of the differences between initiating a relationship online and in a face-to-face situation may be the depth and breadth of self disclosure. People are able to tell an online partner many details about their past and present before they agree to meet, although the accuracy of this information may prove to be a stumbling block for continuing the relationship once they have actually met (McKenna et al., 2002).

Despite these new forms of dating and obtaining sexual pleasure, a substantial minority of young people do not engage in dating and premarital sex. In cultural communities that prefer arranged marriages, social activities continue to occur within a mixed-age community, which enables parents to monitor young people's behaviour and to prevent them from forming inappropriate couple relationships. Other cultural groups permit dating but believe that sex before marriage is risky, culturally unacceptable, or violates religious doctrine. A number of fundamentalist Christian groups, especially in the United States, have successfully encouraged substantial numbers of young people to take public vows of 'purity' and 'chastity' and to delay sexual intercourse (but not necessarily other forms of sexuality) until after marriage. These examples show that considerable diversity remains in patterns of partnering.

What has social research concluded about attractiveness and desirability in intimate partnerships? Generally, researchers have found patterns in partner choices for dating, cohabitation, and marriage but these vary substantially by gender, sexual preference, and culture, and these patterns are changing over time. Characteristics considered desirable and practices felt to be necessary by our parents may now appear old-fashioned or overly rigid and gendered. In addition, global youth culture seems to be blurring some of the international variations but accentuating generational differences. Nevertheless, partner choice is clearly influenced both by socio-economic factors and by psychological factors, as our overview of family theories suggested in Chapter 1.

Who Marries Whom?

Sociologists have relied on several theoretical approaches to explain how people choose their marital partners in free-choice systems; these are portrayed in Table 2.1. Based on a structural approach, the theory of social **homogamy** suggests that people tend to date and marry those from similar socio-economic, religious, and cultural backgrounds and those from similar age groups. These people usually live in the same neighbourhoods, attend the same schools, join the same clubs, and therefore have more opportunity to meet and socialize together. They also feel comfortable with each other because they share similar social backgrounds, lifestyles, and world views. This explanation, however, cannot say why specific individuals choose each other rather than anyone else from their community of social equals.

Table 2.1   Theories of Mate Selection or Marital Choice

Structural Theories	Psychological Theories	Social Construction Theories	Developmental Theories
People marry those who are similar in age, socio-economic background, religion, and culture, who also happen to live nearby (social homogamy). Patriarchal social structures expect men to be older and taller, to have more education and income, and to be the dominant decision-maker.	People marry those they think will complement their psychological needs (complementary needs). People marry partners who subconsciously remind them of parents, siblings, or 'significant others' from the past.	Initial attraction is based on personal and cultural ideals about desirable mates, including those gained from popular heroes and media representations.	Marriage decisions are influenced by emotional advances and retreats, negotiation between partners, conflict resolution skills, and chance factors, as well as social pressure from parents and friends.

Source: Derived from a variety of sources discussed in Baker (2001b).

A variation of the structural theory argues that the ideal heterosexual partnership in a patriarchal and capitalist society requires the male to be older, taller, and more successful occupationally because he is expected to be the breadwinner, main decision-maker, and family representative in the community. The woman is expected to be smaller, attractive, and congenial, but not necessarily well-educated or a high earner because her main role is to raise children and maintain the home even if she also earns some household money. Although the laws in Western societies usually give men and women equal rights, vestiges of patriarchy continue in domestic relations. Many individuals are unaware that they are choosing partners based on these ideals because they have internalized patriarchal gender relations.

Based on the psychoanalytic approach, the theory of complementary needs (Winch, 1955) argues that psychological variables are more important than structural or socio-economic ones in determining attraction and mate selection. Rather than choosing a partner like themselves, people select someone with a different personality, who they think will complement their emotional needs, including the need for attention, care, love, deference, or social status. If two people have equally powerful personalities and are very successful occupationally, their 'egos' might clash. If one is eager to get ahead in the world while the other is more concerned about being supportive and kind, then these two people may find each other attractive and compatible marriage partners.

Another psychological theory suggests that choosing a life partner involves searching for one's ideal mate, who sometimes resembles our opposite-sex parent. Even though young people often vow that they will never marry anyone like their mother or father, they sometimes subconsciously pair up with someone remarkably similar. A more sociological variation of the ideal mate theory suggests that images of desirable partners are socially constructed, including both positive and negative characteristics of opposite-sex parents, older siblings, and experiences with previous partners. In addition, media representations, including fashion magazines, videos, and advertising, increasingly focus on sexuality, youth, and beauty, especially for women. Many people internalize these idealized images even though they are designed to increase consumption.

Developmental theories of mate selection, based on the idea that relationships are negotiated as well as socially constructed, argue that the development of 'courtship' is predetermined by neither social nor psychological variables. Instead, who one marries is the end product of a series of interpersonal interactions characterized by disclosing more personal information, but also advances and retreats, changing definitions of the situation, negotiations, resolution of tensions, and chance encounters. People may meet unexpectedly and find each other good company, but the path to greater commitment and finally to marriage has been portrayed as similar to an escalator. Once you step on, it is difficult not to ride to the top because interpersonal and social pressure to enhance commitment comes in various forms. One partner might persuade the other that living together rather than separately would be more desirable, easier, and cheaper. Alternatively, one partner may receive a job offer in another city and request the other to follow, leading to cohabitation or legal marriage. Relatives and friends might pressure a cohabiting couple to legalize their relationship and once wedding plans are made, they are difficult to cancel even if one partner has second thoughts.

Many young people in Western countries insist that they marry for 'love' but sociologists always argue that 'love' is socially constructed, shaped by interaction and negotiation, gendered practices, socio-economic circumstances, and cultural beliefs. Usually, we 'fall in love' according to implicit gendered and class-based ideals of attractiveness and appropriate partners, as well as considering our personal values and needs. In addition, this tends to happen at a similar stage in the life cycle as our peers, such as when we complete our education and find regular employment. Nevertheless, the ways that we locate our partners and our ideas about acceptable sexual behaviour before marriage have certainly changed throughout the decades. Social activities operate under less parental or community supervision as more young people seem to engage in entertainment involving music, dancing, alcohol, drugs, and sexuality that lasts well into the night. Efforts to find heterosexual and same-sex partners are now more explicit, 'recreational sex' is more open, and the search for new partners now operates in public places, newspapers, and the Internet.

More individuals now have intimate relationships at an early age and experience several sexual relationships before marriage, while some remain chaste until marriage or for life. More couples cohabit before legal marriage, many delay marriage until they reach 28 to 30 years of age, and more avoid legal marriage altogether compared to young people in the 1960s and 1970s. An Australian study indicates that legal marriage remains popular among most people in that country but especially among people over 40 years old, fundamentalist Christians, non-Christian religious groups, and Asian immigrants (Dempsey and De Vaus, 2004). Canadian statistics show that religion still matters in the choice of marriage partner. For example, over 90 per cent of respondents who were Muslim, Hindu, or Sikh, and over 80 per cent of Catholics and Jews, married partners of the same religion, as Table 2.2 indicates (Clark, 2006).

Sociologists continue to find patterns in 'personal choices' and these suggest that gender, age, social class, religion, and culture still influence people's choices about dating, cohabitation, and marriage. Yet, the very existence of greater cultural and lifestyle diversity in urban areas makes it easier for individuals to follow their preferences; however, those who remain living in remote regions simply have fewer choices and may therefore settle on a familiar neighbour rather than an 'ideal' mate. Others choose to avoid marriage altogether.

Table 2.2   Religion of Partners in Conjugal Unions in Canada, 2006

Religion of Respondent	% of Partners Reporting Same Religion
Catholic	84.0
Protestant	78.7
No religion	74.7
Christian	82.3
Orthodox Christian	74.3
Muslim	91.4
Jewish	82.6
Hindu	91.2
Buddhist	80.8
Sikh	96.9
Other religions	54.5
Eastern religions	72.6

Source: Adapted from Clark (2006).

The Single Life

In recent decades, remaining single has taken on new meaning, but a smaller percentage of the population now reaches middle age without marrying, compared to a century ago. Although it is difficult to find statistics that are exactly comparable, we know that 10 per cent of Canadian women in 1900 had never married by the age of 50 compared to seven per cent of women who had never been married by the ages 50–54 in 1996 (Dumas and Péron, 1992; Beaujot, 2000: 103). In Australia, only 4.7 per cent of people have never married by age 75 (ABS, 2007). In many countries, marriage rates increased until the 1970s and then declined again as more people began to cohabit in the 1980s and 1990s. Current marriage rates remain at higher levels than in 1900 but more never-married people now live with a partner or have had sexual experience than in 1900.

Several factors lie behind the larger single and celibate population a century ago. Despite the importance of marriage for social status and economic survival, social rules discouraged people from marrying if they fell in love with someone considered to be an inappropriate marriage partner—such as a person already married or one from another religious or cultural group. Others failed to marry because they were running the family farm or caring for elderly parents and experienced few opportunities to meet potential partners. Early in the twentieth century, more people lived in remote rural areas and small communities and most did not travel as far from home for education or work. Consequently, many could not find a suitable partner within their home communities. Others entered religious orders that required celibacy, a choice that might have been made by some women who preferred a career over marriage and children. In addition, two world wars, by killing thousands of young men, created a shortage of eligible males, and some women could not be satisfied marrying anyone else after losing their fiancés.

Generally, marriage and child-rearing are encouraged by family, friends, and state officials because they are seen as synonymous with maturity, heterosexual identity, and social responsibility. In addition, marriage and reproduction are thought to help individuals retain permanent employment, remain law-abiding, and develop stable relationships and communities. In early settler societies such as Canada, the United States, Australia, and New Zealand, unmarried men were viewed as a threat to community life because they had higher rates than married men of heavy drinking, gambling, and other anti-social activities (Bradbury, 2005). Sexually active but unmarried women were also assumed to threaten family values, although at the same time chaste women were stigmatized as virginal, unwanted, and limited in their life experiences. Ironically, single women in the nineteenth century had more legal rights and better employment opportunities than married women, even though their occupational advancement and social freedom were restricted more than men's. However, legal marriage and child-rearing continue to provide respectability and social status both to men and to women, and to encourage them to spend more time at home within their nuclear families.

Nevertheless, living alone has become easier in the twenty-first century, with urban facilities, household labour-saving devices, greater autonomy and freedom given to those living outside marriage, and more women earning their own living. Single individuals typically experience different lifestyles than married people. They are more likely to rent than to own their home, to eat out in restaurants, to travel abroad, and to seek entertainment outside the home. At the same time, unpartnered men and women tend to maintain closer relationships with their parents and siblings than married people, who are often preoccupied with their spouse and children (Connidis, 2009).

Single women also experience more stable career patterns and higher earnings than married women (Beaujot, 2000). This reflects the fact that single women tend to acquire more formal education and less often take employment leave, as married women more often do in order to move with a husband's job or to raise children. Nevertheless, compared to single men, unmarried women seldom achieve such high-status or well-paid positions as men, who tend to receive their education in different fields, to achieve more prestigious positions, and to receive higher pay than women. Even when they remain single, females are less likely to be encouraged by their bosses, friends, and relatives to excel in paid work, and employment practices often assume that men are more committed or qualified (O'Connor et al., 1999; OECD, 2007a).

Although singleness and childlessness among women have been associated with higher levels of education and occupational success, singleness among men has been related to lower education and lower employment rates than for married men (Beaujot, 2000; Koropeckyj-Cox and Call, 2007). This suggests that remaining single permits both men and women to follow atypical gender paths. For women, this may mean uninterrupted careers, but for men, opting out of marriage reduces their obligations to earn money to support a family. This offers men more opportunities for leisure pursuits or alternative lifestyles, part-time work or self-employment, career changes, retraining, and continuing education.

At all periods in time some single men and women have remained celibate, such as those who join certain religious orders or live in remote areas, but we can no longer assume that never-married people refrain from intimacy and sexual activity. Some single people engage in covert relationships, attempting to protect themselves from the risk of public disapproval because their partner is gay or lesbian, or married to someone else. However, most single people introduce their sexual partners to family as well as friends, even though these people might mistakenly see these relationships as a prelude to marriage.

Some unmarried people have a series of intimate relationships throughout their lives but never settle into long-term cohabitation. This might represent an attempt to create a life free from domestic responsibilities or it could indicate problems with maintaining intimate relationships. Others live in marriage-like relationships but never legally marry. Official statistics tend to blur these distinctions when they label people as 'never married', but some governments are now gathering separate statistics for cohabiting couples. This permits researchers to search for differences between singles who cohabit and those who do not, as well as between cohabiters and married people. However, it will still be difficult to distinguish between those living alone who are celibate and those with active sex lives.

Remaining single or childless is often said to bring loneliness in later life, but single people often remain socially active, retain close contact with siblings and parents, travel widely, and belong to more clubs and organizations than married people (Connidis, 2009). Furthermore, single lifestyles are more socially acceptable now than they used to be, because the age of marriage has increased, marriage rates have declined, separation and divorce rates remain high, and cohabitation has become more prevalent (Sarantakos, 1996: 64–5). In addition, same-sex networks and singles organizations offer social support for those living outside family households. These factors contribute to raising the quality of life for singles and create more public acceptance of non-family lifestyles.

Single people tend to report lower levels of life satisfaction than married people, although this seems to be changing as the attitude towards singleness becomes more positive among younger people. Several studies have indicated that unmarried men report more health problems and lower levels of well-being, and showed that statistically these unmarried men experience higher premature death rates than married men and than all women (De Vaus, 2002; Waite, 2005). These data suggest either that some unhealthy, unhappy, and anti-social men never marry or that the institution of marriage is particularly beneficial to men. Kaufman and Goldsheider (2007) found that both men and women in the United States believe that men need to be married more than women do. However, younger, more educated, and less religious people are less likely to link marriage with life satisfaction.

With age, friends and relatives usually give up trying to 'marry off' their single friends and never-married people learn how to reply to questioning remarks about their single status. Many have developed networks of friends in similar circumstances, who normalize living alone and emphasize the lifestyle advantages, such as higher disposable incomes (for men), more opportunities to travel, time to devote to career (for women), and spontaneity in leisure pursuits. Pressure to marry and bear children tends to lessen after people pass the age when their cohort has married, and especially after women reach menopause.

High levels of life satisfaction are related to perceptions of social support and the maintenance of intimate relationships, which contribute to satisfaction regardless of sexual preference or marital status. Married people can be lonely, lack trust in their partner, have few friends, and experience little social support (Dykstra and Fokkema, 2007). Generally, single people are forced to become more gregarious than married people and many have developed a wider network of acquaintances and friends. Nevertheless, considerable social pressure is still placed on them to marry, even in later life. Well-meaning married friends and relatives sometimes treat single people as less fortunate, lonely, or in need of matchmaking, and these attitudes and pressures reduce their life satisfaction.

Conclusion

In today's urban society, living outside marriage is increasingly feasible and desirable, although two incomes can certainly purchase a better living standard, especially when one is earned by a man. Nevertheless, remaining single has become easier with urban apartment living and household labour-saving devices. Full-time employees can now save time with 'fast food', same-day dry cleaning and laundry services, housecleaning services, handyman services, dishwashers, vacuum cleaners, microwave ovens, and automatic banking machines. In addition, liberal social and sexual attitudes and more effective birth control have enabled more people to enjoy a satisfying sexual life outside traditional marriage. However, less than 10 per cent of people avoid marriage altogether.

Most young people, especially those living in smaller communities and rural areas, expect to find a partner, establish a household together, and produce children; but the timing of these events still depends on their gender, their educational attainment, social class background, and culture. Women still marry at younger ages than men, to men slightly older than themselves, and this age gap grows larger with subsequent marriages. In some cultural communities, women are encouraged to marry well before the median national marriage age, especially if they are immigrants from countries that prefer arranged marriages.

Post-secondary education has become more important in finding work, and those who prolong their education usually remain at home with their parents longer than early school leavers. Young people who find steady work earlier also tend to leave home, cohabit, marry, and reproduce at younger ages. However, more young people from low-income families now attend university with scholarships and loans, and more women graduate from university and move into professional or business positions. Nevertheless, educational and occupational choices are still influenced by gendered and cultural notions of appropriate work as well as by class-based aspirations and opportunities, and economic conditions in the larger society.

The distinction between being 'married' and 'never married' has been blurred in recent years by more liberal sexual behaviour and the practice of cohabiting without a legal ceremony. The social and legal importance of marriage will probably continue to subside as living arrangements are seen more as personal choices than as sacraments or unions regulated by religion or government. In the next chapter, we will examine more closely the differences between cohabitation and legal marriage.

Summary

Over the decades, young people have been given more freedom to choose their intimate partners, although parental and social expectations persist in regard to the social and economic significance of legal marriage, who is considered an appropriate partner, and the importance of public commitment. The chapter also relates changes in sexual behaviour and dating practices to improvements in birth control, the changing status of women, and media representations about sexuality.

Questions for Critical Thought —————

1. Do any aspects of the double standard of sexual behaviour and attitudes still exist? Can women have as many sexual partners as men without social repercussions?

2. Is mate selection still socially regulated in any way? What patterns are evident in current choices about dating and marital partners?

3. Has the single life become more socially desirable in recent years or do most young people still want a permanent partner by midlife?

Suggested Readings

Bogle, Kathleen. 2008. *Hooking Up: Sex, Dating, and Relationships on Campus*. New York: New York University Press. This book is based on qualitative interviews with American middle-class white college students about their sexual practices and dating relationships.

Ward, Peter. 1990. *Courtship, Love, and Marriage in Nineteenth-Century English Canada*. Montreal and Kingston: McGill-Queen's University Press. Through analysis of letters, diaries, and public records, Ward shows that courtship and marriage in nineteenth-century English Canada were influenced by social, institutional, and family constraints.

Wilson, Sue J. 2009. 'Partnering, Cohabitation and Marriage', in M. Baker, ed., *Families: Changing Trends in Canada*, 6th edn. Toronto: McGraw-Hill Ryerson, pp. 68–90. This chapter describes the way that people develop intimate relationships, noting changes in sexual behaviour, dating patterns, and cohabitation as well as practices within legal marriage.

Suggested Websites

Centre for Research on Families and Relationships *www.crfr.ac.uk*
This consortium of researchers in the United Kingdom is based at the University of Edinburgh. Their website contains information about current research projects.

Plentyoffish.com *www.plentyoffish.com*
This is an example of a free online dating service, which can also be used by researchers to analyze how people present themselves to others and what kind of partners they want.

Chapter 3

Cohabitation and Marriage

Learning Objectives
- To understand why more people are choosing to cohabit without legal marriage
- To trace changes in the meaning of marriage for specific categories of people
- To explore research findings about trends in commitment, marital satisfaction, conflict, and the durability of marriage

Chapter Outline

This chapter discusses the rise in heterosexual cohabitation, especially among young adults, and growing acceptance of same-sex unions. It also traces changes in the meaning of legal marriage, and discusses various cultural practices in marriage as well as the 'quality' of marriage.

Introduction

In this chapter, I investigate several theoretical arguments and numerous research findings about the changing nature of cohabitation and legal marriage. We need to understand if patterns of commitment, domestic work, child-bearing, and relationship stability differ between these two types of 'marriage'. We want to know how much social change has actually occurred over past decades in both heterosexual and same-sex marriages, and whether cohabiting relationships are as gendered as legal marriage. If responsibilities and workloads differ between male and female partners, what impact does this have on the quality and stability of family relationships and on patterns of paid work and leisure among men and women?

The British sociologist Anthony Giddens (1992) argued that intimacy in postmodern society has been transformed, partly by the separation of sexual activity from reproduction, and this transformation holds the potential for the radical democratization of heterosexual relationships. In response to this claim, numerous scholars, such as Bittman and Pixley (1997) and Jamieson (1998), have argued that more people may want intimate and egalitarian marriages but there is little empirical evidence that heterosexual relationships substantially differ in this respect from a few decades ago. For example, Bittman and Pixley's Australian research contended that the gap is actually growing between our expectations of intimacy and the reality of everyday family life. They argue (as I do) that we have raised our expectations but that the gendered inequalities in domestic life and labour markets often impede and frustrate people's craving for intimacy and self-fulfillment. Let us examine some of these arguments further by investigating the nature of cohabitation.

Cohabitation among Heterosexual Couples

Cohabiting relationships, or 'consensual unions', have recently become more prevalent and socially acceptable in many Western industrialized countries. Because most governments did not report them in their official statistics until the 1980s, it is difficult to measure longer-term trends. However, we know that cohabiting couples in Canada have increased from 6.3 per cent of all couples in the early 1980s to 15.5 per cent in 2006 (but 34.6 per cent in Quebec) (Wu, 2000: 50; Statistics Canada, 2007d). Australian statistics indicate that cohabiting couples have increased from four per cent of all couples in 1982 (Dempsey and De Vaus, 2004) to 14.9 in 2006 (AIFS, 2008), with 76 per cent of registered marriages involving couples who had previously cohabited (Australian Bureau of Statistics, 2007b). As marriage rates decline, **cohabitation** increases but this living arrangement is more prevalent among younger couples.

About 34 per cent of Canadian women started their conjugal life through cohabitation in 2001 but the figure reached 70 per cent within the province of Quebec (Statistics Canada, 2002b). Le Bourdais and Lapierre-Adamcyk (2004) argue that cohabitation in Quebec, as in Sweden, is nearly indistinguishable from marriage while in the rest of Canada it is still accepted predominantly as a childless phase in conjugal life, as in the United States. Most Canadian cohabiters eventually marry although demographers predict that this will be less likely in the future. Three-quarters of those aged 30 to 39 in 2001 are expected to marry at some point in their lives but 90 per cent of 50- to 69-year-olds were already married in that year (Statistics Canada, 2002b). This suggests that there could be a substantial decline in the percentage of legally married couples in Canada in the future.

The increase in cohabitation rates is linked to many factors. Improvements in birth control have enabled couples to have sexual intercourse without becoming pregnant. More employment opportunities for women have reduced the importance of legal marriage for their financial security. The declining influence of organized religion and the growth of individualism have encouraged couples to follow their own choices rather than social conventions. The cross-national variations in the prevalence of consensual unions also suggest that these rates are influenced by laws, policies, and cultural values.

Cohabiting relationships used to be viewed as temporary arrangements, but as they become more prevalent they look more like marriages. It is not always evident which couples are legally married and which are cohabiting unless you gain personal knowledge about them. They may refer to their 'partner' even when that person is a legal spouse. Some cohabiting women wear a wedding-like ring, while some married women wear no wedding ring and retain their maiden name. If we knew more about these people we might discover that some cohabiting couples share bank accounts while some married couples keep their money separate. Yet despite the similarities, researchers have found important statistical differences between the two types of relationships.

The first difference relates to the relative instability of consensual unions, especially among young people (Ambert, 2005; Bradbury and Norris, 2005; Lichter and Qian, 2008; Qu and Weston, 2008). Statistics Canada reports that first **common-law relationships** are twice as likely to end in separation as first marriages, but that first unions of younger couples are more likely to end in separation than those of older couples regardless of their marital status (Statistics Canada, 2002b). Australian data indicates that cohabiting relationships are three times more likely than legal marriage to end in separation (Qu and Weston, 2008). One reason for the relative instability of cohabitation clearly relates to the youthfulness of people who typically live in these arrangements, but also that cohabiters may differ in some ways from those who never cohabit. Figure 3.1 shows how men's cohabitation rates have increased in Australia and how they are related to age.

Cohabiting partners are also more likely to report no religious affiliation and to have been previously divorced. Dempsey and De Vaus (2004) found that Australian cohabiters recorded in the 1996 and 2001 censuses included more men than women, more people with Anglo backgrounds, fewer Asian immigrants, and fewer people reporting a religious affiliation. Baxter (2002) noted that Australian women in cohabiting relationships were more likely than married women to be employed full-time, to have fewer or no children, and to expect an egalitarian division of labour. Several studies, such as Baxter et al. (2005) and Davis et al. (2007), also showed that cohabiting men do more housework than married men, while cohabiting women do less housework than their married counterparts. American research has found that only a minority of women (15–20 per cent) are involved in multiple cohabitations and that 'serial cohabiters' are over-represented among disadvantaged groups, especially those with low income and education (Lichter and Qian, 2008).

Figure 3.1   Australian Cohabitation Patterns by Age: Percentage of Men Living With a Partner, 1996–2006

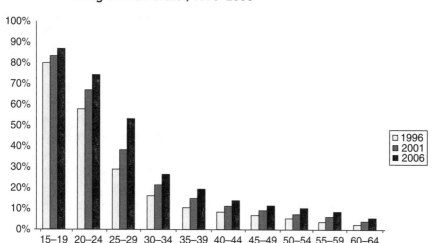

Source: Australian Institute of Family Studies. 2008. *Family Facts and Figures*. Canberra: Commonwealth of Australia (www.aifs.gov.au).

The dramatic increase of cohabitation among young people has prompted sociologists to ask whether this type of relationship merely represents a new form of 'courtship' or whether it signals a fundamental change in commitment or attitudes about marriage. Interpreting cohabitation as a new form of courtship may seem less dangerous from the viewpoint of social conservatives because it predicts that these couples will eventually marry as they mature. If cohabitation actually represents a more fundamental societal change, it may signify a diminishing respect for the church and state and increased emphasis on free choice in personal life, which would predict greater instability in future relationships. These societal changes would require some social adjustments, such as policy reform and new social services.

Researchers have also identified a new kind of relationship they are calling 'living apart together' (LAT). Couples in these relationships may be married but most would be cohabiting, spending allocated days together at regular intervals, such as weekends or holidays, but living apart the rest of the time, sometimes working in different locations. Although figures are unavailable for Canada, about six per cent of 35–44-year-old women in France, and over 10 per cent of 25–34-year-old women in Austria, report being in such a relationship (González-López, 2002). Although some male workers have always worked far away from their homes—especially forestry workers, sailors, and soldiers—more middle-class professional women are now commuting as well. This indicates that living arrangements are becoming more varied but also suggests that employment opportunities continue to influence both family formation and living arrangements.

The Rise in Same-Sex Cohabitation

The rise in cohabitation also includes an increase in same-sex couples living openly together, especially in larger cities, although the official numbers still remain very small. In the 2006 census, only about 0.6 per cent of all couples living together in Canada and Australia were same-sex partners, compared to 0.7 per cent in New Zealand (Statistics Canada, 2007b). However, these figures include only those living in stable relationships who report their status to the census-takers. Some individuals who regularly have same-sex relationships live alone while others may identify as bisexuals and live in heterosexual marriages. American studies suggest that about three per cent of American men and less than two per cent of American women report that their sexual partners are exclusively of the same sex (Black et al., 2000; Ambert, 2005). In addition, Black et al. (2000) estimated that 30 per cent of gay men and 46 per cent of lesbian women had previously been married to heterosexual partners.

Are heterosexual and same-sex couples who share a home different in significant ways? In an Australian study, Sarantakos (1998) found that many of the gay and lesbian couples he studied did not differ significantly from heterosexual couples although they displayed less allegiance to **monogamy** and permanent relationships and less conventionality in sexual identity. Patterson (2000) found that same-sex couples who share a household in the United States report a more egalitarian division of labour than married heterosexual couples. In the American research by Kurdeck (1998, 2001), gay couples reported more autonomy in their activities, friendships, and decision-making than heterosexual married couples. They also reported less approval of their relationships from their birth families, lower levels of commitment between the couple, and higher rates of relationship dissolution than heterosexual couples. Ambert (2005) discusses a number of American studies that indicate gay men show less commitment to monogamy than either lesbians or heterosexual couples. However, she also notes that cohabiting heterosexual partners showed less commitment to monogamy than married partners, although women are more monogamous than men.

Some same-sex couples are happy to share a home without any legal recognition, but this means that if one partner is rushed to the hospital, the other might not have any visiting privileges if he or she is not legally defined as a 'spouse' or a 'family member'. If the couple has children, the other partner may not be seen as a 'parent' by school officials, doctors, or immigration officers. In many countries, same-sex couples have fought for certain forms of legal recognition, including acknowledgement as a 'spouse', permission to marry, and equal access to assisted reproduction services, child-fostering, and adoption (McNair et al., 2002; Weeks, 2002; Ambert, 2005). As we will see in the next section, these issues remain controversial and have generated strong opposition from some religious groups and social conservatives.

The Social and Policy Implications of Increased Cohabitation

The rise in consensual unions has given policy-makers cause for considerable debate. First, they have had to decide whether these relationships should be considered similar to or different from legal marriage in terms of spousal entitlements and obligations (Wu, 2000). One entitlement we mentioned is being considered 'next of kin' if the partner is in an accident or in hospital. Another is to be eligible as a beneficiary to the partner's health insurance plan or retirement benefits. Secondly, if couples separate acrimoniously and ask the courts to divide their shared assets, should the state proceed in the same manner as for legal marriages? In many countries, legal reforms already require the equal division of family assets when marriage partners separate, unless doing so would create inequity or unfairness, but this legislation does not always cover cohabiting couples.

Although some cohabiting couples want more legal rights, others choose to keep their personal arrangements outside any legal requirements. They may see cohabitation as a private choice that involves less commitment, fewer obligations to their partner or his/her kin group, a less gendered division of labour, and the option to leave without complications when the relationship is no longer mutually beneficial (Barber and Axinn, 1998; Elizabeth, 2000). Alternatively, they may see no practical advantage to legalizing their relationship or they may believe that the church and state have no right to intervene in their personal lives. The lack of legal protection, however, has sometimes left female partners with fewer assets and less income after separation. This is especially relevant for a cohabiting couple with children, where one partner has supported the family financially while the other (usually the woman) has provided unpaid domestic services and child care. If the relationship ends, these mothers and children could become impoverished unless the fathers continued to support them, the mothers were able to find well-paying work, or the state supplemented their incomes.

Some governments have resolved these issues by deeming heterosexual couples to be 'married' in terms of their rights, responsibilities, and the division of their joint assets after living together for a specified time (usually between one and three years, depending on the jurisdiction). If partners do not wish to divide their property equally upon future separation, they must sign a legal contract to specify alternative arrangements. However, all states agree that parents must support any children they produce, whether or not parents are legally married or living with the children.

Some countries or jurisdictions have recently changed their laws and regulations about these issues, while others continue to debate them. A number of jurisdictions, including New Zealand, have created a new category of relationship called a **civil union**, which provides some legal recognition and rights for those cohabiting couples who are either same-sex or heterosexual and choose to go this route. Civil unions may not share all of the same rights as legal marriage but their creation represents a political compromise that offers some legal protection while respecting the traditional idea that marriage is a legal partnership between a man and a woman (Moore, 2003). Other jurisdictions (such as Canada) have simply allowed same-sex couples the same marriage rights as heterosexual couples enjoy.

Belgium and the Netherlands legalized civil unions in 2001 (Arie, 2003). In 2003, the Canadian government drafted legislation to permit **same-sex marriage** but the legality of this bill was immediately challenged and sent to the Supreme Court of Canada. In December 2004 the Supreme Court of Canada unanimously determined that the federal government has the right to redefine marriage to include same-sex couples. This meant that federal and provincial laws and regulations had to be amended, and the federal Civil Marriages Act of July 2005 formally legalized same-sex marriage. However, in the 2006 census, only 17 per cent of the 45,350 same-sex couples in Canada were legally married (VIF, 2007). New Zealand's Civil Union Bill was introduced by the Labour-led government and passed in December 2004 with considerable opposition from religious groups and the (conservative) National Party. This law enables hetero-sexual or same-sex couples to register their unions with the state and acquire partnership rights, which include being considered 'next of kin' if one partner is admitted to a hospital. In return, they would be considered legal partners for purposes of income tax, support obligations, or social benefits but not necessar-ily recognized as legally married 'spouses' by some religious groups or in other countries.

The fight for civil unions and same-sex marriage has been led mainly by social reformers who argue that human rights are violated when long-term same-sex relationships are not acknowledged or respected by the state or employers. However, legalizing same-sex unions has been strongly opposed by a number of religious groups, including the Catholic Church and fundamentalist Christians as well as other social conservatives. Opponents tend to view civil unions and same-sex relationships as threatening to the institution of marriage, to public morality, to Biblical teachings, to stable patterns of reproduction and socializa-tion, and to the norm of heterosexuality.

The rise in cohabitation is perceived by social conservatives as a negative trend, but having children outside legal marriage is considered a potential problem of greater proportions. In most Western industrialized countries, more babies are born outside legal marriage now than in earlier decades, although most are born to cohabiting couples. This dramatic increase in births outside marriage worries some policy-makers because the lower stability rates of these relationships could have negative implications for children's well-being. In Australia, 33 per cent of births in 2007 were to parents who were not in a registered marriage (ABS, 2008).

Canadian figures show that 38 per cent of live births in 2006 were to women who were not married or living with their legal spouse (Statistics Canada, 2008), compared to nine per cent in 1975 and four per cent in 1960 (VIF, 2000, 1994). Notable provincial differences are apparent in the Canadian statistics, with a high of 61.5 per cent of births outside marriage in Quebec and a low of 26 per cent in Ontario in 2006 (Statistics Canada, 2008). The vast majority of these children are born to couples in their twenties and thirties who are cohabiting, but these couples tend to have more stable relationships than younger childless cohabiters (Wu, 1996).

When more couples enter consensual unions, relationships typically become less stable at the national level (Beck-Gernsheim, 2002). If these relationships are unprotected legally, separations could lead to disputes about how assets should be divided, whether financial support should be paid, and where any children born to the couple should live. Cohabiting fathers have a higher probability of separating from their partners than married fathers, and subsequently of losing contact with their children. Goldscheider and Kaufman (1996) argued that although cohabitation usually represents a lower level of commitment to partners, it also means that men are more likely than women to reduce their commitment to children. A father who is not living with his children can have a positive influence on them if he is involved, but a substantial minority of fathers are not involved, as we will see in Chapter 6. Furthermore, his tenuous relationship with the mother on issues of parenting can also bring conflict into the children's lives. Goldscheider and Kaufman argued that more research is needed on the impact on children of parents' commitment to each other.

In a qualitative study in the United Kingdom, Lewis (1999) found that cohabiting and married parents both said that they made commitments to each other and to their children. However, the commitments of cohabiting couples tended to be private, while the married ones were public. The younger generation of parents talked about commitments as personal issues that were internally driven, whereas their own parents talked more about obligations that were externally imposed. Jamieson et al. (2002) found that legal marriage was seen as irrelevant to commitment by many Scottish young people (ages 20–29 years), although some saw legal marriage as important for children.

Cohabitation is viewed by many young people as a good way to test their relationship but cohabitation is less stable than marriage. Furthermore, American researchers have also found lower levels of interpersonal commitment by men but not women in cohabiting relationships (Stanley et al., 2006). They also found that the quality of cohabiting relationships and levels of satisfaction tend to be lower than marriage, but couples who plan to marry tend to have higher relationship quality. Nevertheless, many couples 'slide' from dating to cohabitation in a non-deliberate and incremental way, without fully considering the implications. Stanley et al. (2006) use the words 'sliding versus deciding', which they argue contributes to lower commitment and increases vulnerability in times of stress. Compared to dating, cohabitation encourages couples to remain in relationships that are not fully satisfying but are more complex to end, and these couples could also slide into unsatisfactory marriages.

Cohabiting women in Australia are more likely than legally married women to be employed full-time (Baxter, 2002), which suggests they are more likely to have the financial resources to leave unhappy relationships. Although some cohabiting relationships last a lifetime, most end in separation or legal marriage. One interesting question about these trends relates to why so many of the couples who decide to stay together eventually marry when there appear to be diminishing differences between cohabitation and marriage? Also, why do some cohabiting couples who subsequently marry arrange wedding ceremonies that retain many of the conventional symbols of traditional (patriarchal) marriage? We will try to answer these questions in the next section by providing some historical background on social and legal changes in marriage.

The Changing Meaning of Marriage

Despite the increasing similarities between cohabitation and legal marriage, they are still perceived as different by many people, especially lawyers, government officials, parents, and older relatives. Legal marriage is seen as a public, long-term commitment to another person, with accompanying legal rights and obligations, while cohabitation is more often seen as a transitional status involving lower levels of commitment. Although many cohabiting couples make private commitments to each other, decisions to marry after a period of cohabitation might signal a desire to make a public commitment before parents and friends and to celebrate this important decision and transition (Lewis, 1999; Pryor, 2005).

A decision to legally marry might also represent a desire to produce children together with assurance that they will be considered 'legitimate' by their grandparents and other relatives, as well as by the law. In addition, marriage after cohabitation could represent an attempt to gain legal protection in case of guardianship problems with children, of illness or disability that could draw on the partner's insurance, of immigration problems when moving across international borders, or of inheritance problems if one partner dies prematurely. Some of these issues seem more relevant for older people, which may partly explain why they are more likely than younger couples to legally marry.

Historically, both the church and the state viewed marriage as an economic and sexual partnership between husbands and wives that involved mutual dependency in the common endeavours of earning a living and raising

of the man and woman as well as the names of parents, uncles, aunts and their occupations, qualifications and even property ownership. This forms the basis of the first screening and is done without personal meetings to avoid a 'loss of face' if an alliance does not materialize. Once the screening is completed, the family elders meet and 'size up' the other party for marriage compatibility. The prospective bride and groom are then introduced to each other and, if all goes well, become engaged. After several meetings and gift exchanges, they are married in a ceremony that symbolizes the union of two families rather than two individuals.

When I turned 20, my grandmother from India enthusiastically undertook the responsibility of finding me a husband. Until then, my life revolved around a government job and university study while my parents worked in Australia. Some of my friends had Indian backgrounds but others were New Zealanders with European, Maori, and Pacific Island backgrounds. My girlfriends and I regularly discussed heterosexual relationships and were open to the possibility of finding the 'right man'.

Once I turned 20, I began receiving *ism navesis* and photos of young men by e-mail and normal mail, accompanied by a letter or phone call from India from my grandmother, uncle, or aunt eliciting my feedback. At first I found the process humorous but also puzzling. How was I supposed to guess a man's virtue or suitability from a photograph or resumé? My friends and I used to discuss the man's attributes before dismissing them for real or imagined incompatibilities. I didn't think the process would come to much, given the unlikelihood that 'suitors' would be sent to meet me in Auckland.

One day they sent a photograph of a 28-year-old man with a university degree, who ran a computer training institute in India, and who I had met as a child because he was the son of my grandmother's cousin. The photo showed a man sitting on a sofa wearing an intense expression and for once I was unable to find any reasons to reject him. I reluctantly agreed to accept his phone call and one call led to another and then to an online chat. However, within six months our wedding date had been set in India. The news shocked me because unconsciously I was still expecting a romantic relationship to develop first. When I spoke to my uncle about how sudden

(Continued)

Box 3.1 Continued

it all seemed and how I was unprepared to go through with a wedding, he was aghast at my concept of a developing relationship and my Western ideas seemed quite foreign to him.

This conversation led to weeks of family pressure about how I would bring 'dishonour' to my family if I didn't go through with the wedding, and would insult the man's family after they had 'given their word' for the alliance. Since I didn't have any problem with the man in question, my relatives argued, why was I opposed to marrying him? By then I understood that their version of marriage involved love and commitment growing out of marriage while in the Western version, love and commitment came first. If I agreed to marry this man, I would be committed for life without even meeting him and would have to trust the family that the marriage would work out despite the culture gap and probable differences in our expectations. If I refused to marry him, I would be insulting a family who felt they were acting in my best interests. I also realized that choosing my own partner would provide no guarantee of a happy lasting relationship.

Ten days before my wedding, I reached India and found my grandparents' sprawling home full of relatives, cooks, tailors, jewellers, and others preparing for the wedding. The next day, I met my fiancé—Ayub. It was a strange meeting to say the least. Our phone and e-mail conversations had been private but this meeting included his mother, two sisters, and three aunts. I felt like I was on display and had to gain their approval. These ladies seemed very nice but asked personal and probing questions such as: Will you work after getting married? Do you cook? What do you do in your spare time? I was shocked at the personal questions but should have realized that the relatives have the right to voice their opinions about the potential partner in an arranged marriage system. However, I never had a decent look at Ayub, nor did I meet him alone, until we were married!

The wedding was a long process involving ceremonial visits and gift exchanges. Some gifts included jewellery and ornate clothes so I didn't have much to complain about. Muslim marriages also involve a marriage contract, in which the bride (or her male representative) stipulates

(Continued)

conditions, such as money or property, that the husband is obliged to give her in the event of separation or divorce. Once the contract is signed, the marriage is complete and a reception or feast takes place. The next hurdle is the celebration of the marriage consummation, which by Muslim law should take place as soon as possible. The rationale behind this I think is that if one finds the other lacking in some respect, then the differences could be ironed out while the guests are able to help resolve the issue.

I need not have worried because my husband was very unlike the stereotypical Indian Muslim male I expected. He was articulate, pleasant, well-read, had very balanced ideas about gender roles that matched my own, and was willing to live in New Zealand. So the result has been that despite my misgivings and my friends' doubts, my husband and I have been happily married for the last four years and have a three-year-old son. I believe now that some arrangements are made in heaven!

Source: Reprinted with the permission of Nargis Ali, 17 November 2008, Auckland, New Zealand.

Immigrants living in westernized countries might encourage their young people to return home to their place of origin in order to marry a partner already selected by family members still living there. Increasingly, young people expect to exercise some personal choice over their marriage partner or at least to acquire veto rights, especially if they live abroad, have obtained a Western education, or have travelled in Western countries. However, young people may also be pressured to abide by the marriage decisions of their elders, especially if they live in remote rural areas, have little formal education, or little means of support outside their family's assets.

In Asian and African countries with arranged marriage systems, parents sometimes make pre-marriage agreements or even child betrothals with other parents before their children reach puberty. These arrangements, which could be initiated when the children are under the age of 10, are sometimes seen as legal contracts that cannot easily be broken without some form of compensation between families. Making such promises early in their children's lives precludes less desirable marriage choices and prevents inappropriate love or sexual attachments from developing among young people (ibid.).

In arranged marriage systems, greater importance is placed on financial security, potential heirs, and extended family solidarity than on sexual attraction or love between the bride and groom. Potential marital partners are urged to respect each other and their family's wishes, and it is hoped that love will develop after partners marry and share a home. Both families maintain a stake in marital stability, so it is not surprising that arranged marriages less often end in divorce than is the case with free-choice unions. However, in these countries, divorce is often legally restricted, sometimes making it easier for men to divorce their wives than for women to divorce their husbands. In addition, women might be motivated to make the marriage work if they cannot support themselves outside marriage or must forfeit child guardianship rights to the husband or his relatives in a divorce. Increasingly, young people throughout the world are encouraged to seek a more intensive and egalitarian relationship through the influence of Western education, international travel, foreign films, popular music, the Internet, and global advertising.

In Western countries, the law requires the consent of both bride and groom before a wedding can take place. Young people usually meet their future spouse in school, at work, at community functions, or somewhere in their neighbourhood. Friends and relatives may offer assistance by introducing potential partners but individuals make their own marriage choices based on their perceptions of compatibility and feelings of physical attraction and love. Similar interests and cultural backgrounds are valued in partners yet other social and gendered ideas also influence our decisions, as we already discussed in Chapter 2.

Despite the apparent differences between arranged marriages and free-choice marriages, decisions are influenced by some of the same considerations. In Western marriages, couples expect to marry for 'love' but at the same time people marry for a variety of reasons, including companionship, emotional stability, regular and safe sex, the desire for children, and additional financial support. Being acknowledged as an adult and establishing a separate residence from parents may also be motivations for marriage, as the wedding is still considered an adult 'rite of passage' or social acknowledgement of the attainment of adult status, even when the couple has been living together. Love can certainly develop and thrive outside legal marriage, which suggests that people in all cultures marry for more than love.

Preferred Marriage Partners and the Exchange of Gifts

Some Eastern and African cultures have established preferential marriage rules that stipulate certain categories of people as the most socially desirable partners. In southern India, the cross-cousin or the child of the mother's brother or father's sister is considered to be the most desirable marriage partner, which helps to cement together the two families (Nanda and Warms, 2007). Some countries permit more than one spouse at a time (called polygamy) although the typical pattern is for men to marry more than one wife (polygyny) but not for women to take multiple husbands (polyandry). Most polygamous countries do not permit men with insufficient financial resources to marry a second wife, which means that polygamy remains a status symbol for wealthier men. Additionally, in some polygamous cultures, tradition specifies that a man should marry the widow of his dead brother even if he already has a partner (ibid.). This practice, called the levirate, provides some means of support for widows in cultures that do not encourage women to earn their own living. Marriage to a wife's sister (sororate) is encouraged in other cultures, especially if the first wife is infertile or dies prematurely. These customs indicate that marriage is conceptualized as a union or alliance between kin groups rather than as an intimate relationship between individuals (ibid.).

One legal spouse at a time is the law and custom in all Western countries, where 'bigamy'—marrying two partners simultaneously—is a criminal offence. The state's requirement of a marriage licence represents an attempt to eliminate bigamy, as does the Christian tradition of 'reading the banns', or announcing the forthcoming wedding in church for three consecutive Sundays to see if anyone knows of any impediment to the marriage. The waiting period between obtaining the marriage licence and celebrating the wedding ceremony may be a few days to several weeks, which is designed to discourage hasty marriages. Now that legal divorce has been made easier to obtain in many places, an increasing percentage of the population marries more than once over a lifetime, referred to as **serial monogamy**.

In cultures with arranged marriage systems, dowries have sometimes been used to attract a partner for daughters, to cement alliances between families, and to help establish new households. Dowries involve payments of money or gifts of property that usually accompany brides into marriage and become part of marriage agreements. Although the types of payment vary considerably, they might include household furnishings, jewels, money, servants, farm or pack animals, or land. If a woman has a large dowry, she can find a 'better' husband, which usually means one who is wealthier, healthier, better educated, and from a more respected family. In some cultures, the dowry money becomes the property of the groom's family and in others it is used to establish the bride and groom's new household. Dowries have also been used to provide brides with some measure of financial security or insurance in case of partner abuse, divorce, or widowhood, but how effective this practice is depends on how much control women have over the money or property (Barker, 2003).

In **patrilocal systems** where the bride and groom reside with his family, the dowry money would make an important contribution to the household of the groom's parents. Clearly, this system encourages families to prefer sons over daughters, because males can bring new resources into the household through marriage settlements, males can more easily support the family through employment, and males also perpetuate the family name. Consequently, female fetuses have been aborted and female children and adults have been neglected or mistreated because of the economic stresses perpetuated in the dowry system. This system penalizes families with few resources if they must provide money or property in order to secure a husband for their daughter(s) but have no or few sons to attract dowries. For these reasons, dowries have been outlawed in some countries, such as India, although even there they continue to operate clandestinely in rural areas (Nanda and Warms, 2007).

In other cultures, the groom's kin group has been expected to pay a 'bride price' to gain permission to marry the family's daughter, to establish and secure alliances, and to compensate for the bride's lost labour or child-bearing potential in her birth community (Fleising, 2003). This pattern has been more prevalent in subsistent horticultural economies (such as sub-Saharan Africa), in patrilineal societies, and in places where the bride customarily moves to the groom's community. However, dowries and bride prices are disappearing as both men and women become educated and westernized, as more people live in urban areas, and as women gain opportunities to enter the labour force and become self-supporting.

Symbolic remnants of dowries and bride prices remain in traditional free-choice marriages, even in Western countries. Trousseaus or 'glory boxes' consisting of special household items and fancy clothing are still collected by some girls and/or their families for their new home, their weddings, and the 'honeymoon'. Grooms sometimes purchase expensive (most often diamond) engagement rings to assure their fiancées' consent to marry and give (usually gold) wedding bands during the ceremony (although sometimes both partners exchange rings). Brides and their families generally make most of the wedding arrangements and sometimes pay for the reception meal, while grooms and their families often pay for drinks at the reception and for the wedding trip.

In Western countries, traditional weddings are redolent with symbolism that harks back to traditional practices and values of previous eras. The white wedding dress represents the virginity that used to be expected of brides. The bride entering the church on the arm of her father who then 'gives her away' to the groom symbolizes the patriarchal exchange of the woman from the authority of one man to another. The throwing of rice or confetti after the ceremony represents the community's wish that the marriage will be fertile and that the couple will be blessed with many children. The sharing of the reception activities and expenses represents the joining together of two families.

Many of these traditions are fading with the rising age of marriage, more remarriages, and opportunities to create individualized wedding ceremonies. The prevalence of remarriages among older partners means that many of the financial costs are now paid by the bride and groom themselves rather than their parents. Although many couples eliminate some traditions from their weddings, a considerable number of couples marry in church, brides wear white dresses and are 'given away' by their fathers, and friends and relatives throw confetti. This may be done even when the couple doesn't attend church, the bride is no longer a virgin and rejects patriarchal practices, and they plan to remain child-free. These wedding practices often represent either a desire to maintain cultural traditions or social pressure to retain some practices, regardless of their original meanings.

Residence, Relations with Kin, and Surnames

Marriage systems sometimes require either the bride or the groom to relocate and live with one kin group, leaving her or his own family of origin behind. Rules of patrilocality and patrilineal descent require the woman to move to the community or home of her husband's family and give priority to his kin group. The important kinship ties are passed from father to son to grandson, which is the most prevalent pattern with a long history in both Eastern and Western civilizations (Leslie and Korman, 1989: 48). Within this system, a wife would marry into her husband's family, and their children would become members of his kin group. With **matrilineal descent**, relationships are traced through the female line, downplaying the importance of the father's relatives. Matrilineal descent and **matrilocality**—living with or near the bride's kin group—were practised by some indigenous people in North America, including the peoples of the Iroquois Confederacy at the time of European contact (Brown, 1988).

If newly married couples are considered to be equal members of both kin groups, called **bilateral descent**, they might participate in the family activities of both the bride and groom and could inherit from either side of the family. Both kin membership and inheritance are based on bilateral descent in most Western countries, but among the British upper classes, primogeniture was the rule for inheritance until well into the twentieth century. This meant that the first-born male child inherited the family home or estate and subsequent children received an annual income or smaller amounts of family resources. This system of inheritance maintained the integrity of large landholdings but encouraged younger sons to move away, take on business or professional jobs, become career military officers, or emigrate. Throughout the colonies, younger sons of wealthy British families emigrated and were known as remittance men, after the regular remittance of allowance that was sent to them. The system also assumed that daughters would marry and be supported by their husbands, although rich daughters often entered marriage with private incomes from their fathers' estates. The system of primogeniture perpetuated legal inequalities that were sometimes resented by sons and daughters.

Upon marriage, surnames have traditionally passed through the male side of the family in the English-speaking or common-law countries, although this was often done through custom rather than law. The bride and the couple's subsequent children took the groom's family name because he was the legal head of the household and his name symbolized their legal and social union. Most couples still maintain this pattern because it seems easier, they think it is a legal requirement, or they feel that one name acknowledges their legal union. However, a name change may mean that the bride loses her professional identity or acquaintances who did not know of her marriage or her new name. In Quebec, married women are legally required to keep their birth names, although they may add their husband's surname to it, but in Ontario brides may choose either their (father's) surname or their husband's at the time of marriage (Baker, 2001b). In addition, anyone may create a new name by going through a legal name change or simply by adopting a new name, as long as this is not done for fraudulent purposes.

Since the 1970s, more women have retained their birth name after marriage. This is sometimes a professional decision for those who want to maintain a profile with colleagues, customers, or (in the case of politicians or public performers) their followers or fans. It might also be a feminist statement about unwillingness to lose a former identity. A few women actually choose new surnames that do not relate to their father or husband. However, many women continue to take their husbands' name upon marriage, often to the surprise of professional colleagues and kin. This may involve a conscious effort to discard a difficult or unpopular name, or a public statement about being married as opposed to cohabiting, or a statement about their unity in marriage. Furthermore, some people feel that life would be too complicated with a different name for husband, wife, and children, while some women assume their husband's name because they want to emphasize their new status or rite of passage.

Newly married couples in Western countries usually try to establish a residence apart from both kin groups after marriage, which is called a **neo-local residence**. Most couples prefer this arrangement even if it means accepting a lower living standard and later forgoing live-in child-care services. Although many couples with European backgrounds reside with parents at some point in their marriage, especially when they are in financial difficulty, most would define this living arrangement as a temporary and undesirable hardship. However, certain cultural groups are far more likely to live in extended families, seeing this arrangement as cost-effective, a solution to child-care problems, socially desirable, and culturally appropriate.

These cultural variations indicate that all social groups create customary expectations relating to marriage and weddings, although many of them are unwritten or even unspoken. Such customs evolve over time but individuals sometimes experience family opposition when they try to ignore cultural traditions or attempt to create their own. Both social pressures and the law ensure that couples intending to marry abide by at least some of these rules or practices. Although people have more choice about weddings and marriage partners than they did in the past, they still cannot marry more than one person at a time if they live in a Judeo-Christian country. The law also requires people to reach a certain age in order to marry (the age of majority) and stipulates that some potential partners are unsuitable (close relatives). Declining legal marriage rates suggest that more people are choosing to create their own consensual unions outside of matrimony, but if they legally marry, they often embrace at least some of the traditional practices.

Marriage Rates

Since the 1970s, the crude marriage rates (defined as the number of new marriages in a specified year per 1,000 in the total population) steadily declined in many countries. The decline in legal marriage is often attributed to the rise in informal living arrangements and the fading relevance of legal marriage as a form of financial security (OECD, 2005b: 33). Cross-national differences are apparent in marriage rates but declining rates have created noticeable differences between generations and income groups, with older and wealthier people much more likely to marry.

Marriage rates also fluctuate with the rise and fall in living costs, the availability and cost of residential housing, the pressures of war, employment opportunities, and the availability of contraception. The Canadian marriage rate reached a low point of 5.9 marriages per 1,000 people during the Great Depression of the 1930s because couples could not afford to marry and establish separate households. However, the rate rose sharply during the Second World War, to 10.9, when people had more money and wanted to cement their unions in order to gain emotional security, sexual freedom, and possibly state income support if the husband was killed or injured. After the war, the rate declined until 1961, increased to over nine marriages per 1,000 people in 1971, and then fell again. The Canadian marriage rate continued to decline from 5.5 in 1994 to 4.7 in 2003 as more people cohabited without legalizing their relationship, and has stabilized at that rate (Statistics Canada, 2003; 2007d).

The average age of first marriage has also increased in many countries since the 1970s, influenced by rising educational requirements for employment and higher housing costs. In Canada, the average age of first marriage in the 1960s was 22 years for women and 25 years for men, but this increased to 28.5 for women and 30.6 for men by 2003 (Statistics Canada, 2007d). Because so many people now divorce and remarry, the average age of all marriages in Canada is 31.7 years old for brides and 34.3 for grooms (Statistics Canada, 2003). Table 3.1 shows some marriage statistics for Canada and Australia.

Table 3.1   Marriage Trends in Canada and Australia

Country	Consensual Unions (% of all couples)		Legal Marriage Rate (per 1,000 Population)	Median Age of first Marriage, 2003–2006	
	1991	2006		Brides	Grooms
Canada	6.3	15.5	4.7 (2003)	28.5	30.6
Australia	8.0	14.9	5.5 (2006)	27.6	29.6

Sources: Baker (2001b), VIF (2007), Australian Bureau of Statistics (2007).

The growing secularization of society has encouraged more people to view marriage as a contract that can be broken under certain circumstances. Individualism and the idea that people are entitled to satisfying relationships have discouraged couples from staying together out of duty or concern for family reputation. Furthermore, more effective contraception has permitted people to separate sex and reproduction, and the decline in fertility—with fewer children per family—has made divorce easier. Separation and divorce also became more economically feasible when more women could support themselves from their earnings and when governments began paying income support to low-income households led by mothers. More liberal divorce laws also contributed to rising divorce rates.

Lower marriage rates, declining fertility, and rising divorce rates are viewed by many social conservatives as trends that demonstrate the decline in the family as a social institution. However, others view these trends as indicators of greater choice and personal freedom in society, permitting more people to recreate satisfying relationships. Although legal marriage rates are declining and the age of marriage is rising, most people continue to live in couple relationships. For example, almost three-quarters of Canadian women aged 35–39 years live with a partner, either legally married or cohabiting (Statistics Canada, 2007c). This suggests that 'marriage' remains very popular if we define it in broader terms.

The Quality of Marriage

Researchers have tried to understand why so many people see marriage as a desirable living arrangement. In one popular motif, 'scheming' women are said to push reluctant bachelors into marriage; however, several studies have suggested that men see marriage as desirable and may even benefit more from marriage than women do. Bernard (1972) first popularized the research finding that married men in the United States experience fewer psychiatric problems and less physical illness, and also tend to live longer than single men, but found that this trend was less apparent for women. Bernard argued that men do well in marriage because they have someone to care for them physically and emotionally, to keep their households functioning, and to look after their children. In contrast, women marry at some cost to their own physical and emotional health because they are expected to continually cater to other people's needs as well as to their own.

De Vaus (2002) used this earlier American research as a starting point to see how marriage impacted on the well-being of men and women in Australia. When a range of mental disorders were considered (including mood swings, anxiety, and drug and alcohol abuse), he found that married people were less likely to experience these problems than single people. De Vaus concluded that regardless of whether they are married or not, women are more at risk of mood and anxiety disorders than men, but men are more at risk of drug and alcohol disorders. Marriage and child-rearing do not increase the risk for either men or women. However, married people are less likely to report these problems than never-married or separated/divorced people. Although people with these disorders may be less likely to marry in the first place or to stay married, De Vaus concluded that having a close relationship seems to act as a buffer to health-related problems.

Using recent American data, Waite (2005) demonstrated statistically that on a wide range of indicators of health and well-being, legally married people are healthier, happier, and live longer than never-married people, but only if they rate their relationship as 'moderately good' or 'excellent'. Although acknowledging that unhealthy or unhappy people are less likely to marry and stay married, she also argued that a close intimate relationship assists people to fight against stress and poor health. However, a poor and unsatisfying relationship can damage people's health and well-being.

Marriage satisfaction research is usually based on a cross-sectional design done at one point in time, with few studies following the same couples over periods of more than 10 years. This is because longitudinal studies are expensive and difficult when people move away or withdraw from the research project. However, Karney and Bradbury (1995) surveyed 100 longitudinal studies of marriage from which they created a model to explain why some survive and others dissolve. They called it the 'vulnerability-stress-adaptation' model. These researchers noted that marriage satisfaction and stability are influenced by a combination of individual factors, family variables, and life events. The 'enduring vulnerabilities' are the strengths and weaknesses that each spouse brings to the marriage, influenced by their upbringing, social background, and their attitudes. Stressful life events are incidents, transitions, or circumstances that can impinge on their relationship and create tension or stress. Adaptive processes refer to the ways that people cope with stress and conflict, and how couples communicate and support each other. The authors concluded that the strategies for dealing with life events and resolving conflicts vary by these factors, which then influence marital satisfaction.

Some research suggests that couples married for a long time can impart their wisdom to the younger generation whose marriages are far less likely to last (Parker, 2002). However, the current cohort of young married couples is experiencing very different social, economic, political, and cultural circumstances than those married for many years. Nevertheless, marriage preparation courses and marriage counselling are becoming more prevalent, as therapists, policy-makers, and older couples express increasing concern about high rates of relationship breakdown, especially in the United States. Most of these courses, however, are targeted to those who are planning to marry and those whose marriages have already broken up. Few formal supports exist for ongoing relationships despite the fact that the research suggests that rewarding and lasting marriages require regular and intentional maintenance (ibid.).

Much of the sociological, social work, and policy research about couples deals with conflict rather than durability. These studies find that violence against female partners is surprisingly prevalent and consequential for individuals, families, and the welfare state.

Male Violence against Female Partners

Male violence against female partners seems to be increasing but it may just be reported more often. A Canadian telephone survey found that 29 per cent of women reported physical or sexual abuse by an intimate partner over their lifetime and one-third of these said that they feared for their lives at some point in the relationship (Jaffe et al., 2003: 5). Physical abuse is not usually an isolated event, as some women have been assaulted and have sought help many times from friends, neighbours, social workers, and the police (Johnson, 1990; Leibrich et al., 1995). Adults who abuse their spouses (and children) have a higher probability of coming from families where their parents engaged in similar behaviour, and women who were abused during 'courtship' have a much higher probability of being abused during marriage (O'Leary et al., 1989; Barnes et al., 1991). Furthermore, cohabiting women are more likely than married women to experience partner violence and also severe violence including intimate femicide (Brownridge, 2008). Separated women are more likely than those who are married or divorced to be assaulted and killed by former partners (Wilson and Daly, 1994; Krug et al., 2002: 96; DeKeseredy, 2009). This suggests that remaining in a violent relationship is dangerous for women, but that taking action to escape the violence can also have lethal consequences.

Comparative research suggests that physical abuse within intimate relationships becomes more prevalent when a society condones violence, when violence has become a form of entertainment in films and sports events, and when a country is engaged in war (Krug et al., 2002). Women become more vulnerable to physical, sexual, and emotional abuse if they see their male partner as the 'head of the household' or if they are financially dependent on him and cannot support their children alone (Baker, 2001b: 110). Women are also more vulnerable to abuse if they are cohabiting or are separated from their partner and living in low-income housing developments with other single parents (DeKeseredy, 2005, 2009; Brownridge, 2008). Certain cultural groups, such as indigenous women in Canada, Australia, and New Zealand, report exceptionally high rates of abuse by male partners (McGillvray and Comaskey, 1998; Brownridge, 2003).

Domestic violence programs, operated by both government and private agencies, typically offer crisis intervention, first helping a woman to develop protection plans that could involve laying charges against her partner or former partner. The woman is also helped to find transitional housing for herself and her children, to engage a lawyer, and, if necessary, to apply for income support to cover living expenses. In both individual counselling and group therapy, battered wives are encouraged to view partner abuse as unacceptable regardless of the circumstances or their own behaviour, although most abused women find it difficult to erase lingering feelings that the abuse was somehow their own fault. Male abusers are more often charged with an offence and encouraged (or required) to accept counselling, which includes taking responsibility for their acts of violence rather than blaming their partners. They are also helped to control their emotions, develop better communication skills, learn non-violent behaviour from male role models, and redefine what it means to be a man.

Community agencies and school boards sometimes collaborate to develop violence-prevention strategies focusing on staff development and awareness, community involvement, and student programs (Wolfe and Jaffe, 2001: 290; Mullender et al., 2003: 147). One of the early American programs to promote violence awareness and safety skill development with school-age children was implemented by the Minnesota Coalition for Battered Women. The program targeted elementary and secondary students throughout the state to ensure that all children knew about alternatives to domestic violence (Wolfe and Jaffe, 2001: 290). Action against family violence also includes sensitization workshops for professionals, such as teachers and judges, to increase their knowledge of program options and the personal and social implications of this form of violence (DeKeseredy, 2009). In addition, support services for **at-risk families** have been provided when violence seems to be a possibility because of their stressful circumstances.

Despite these initiatives, Sev'er (2002) concluded that little has changed in the past two decades for urban Canadian women who do not turn to women's shelters. Many women remain in abusive relationships because they do not know where to turn for assistance, because they cannot find temporary and low-income housing, or because they cannot support their children on their own. Tolerance of abuse continues because some women feel that it may somehow be their own fault, while others fear reprisal from partners who threaten to kill them if they go to the police or tell anyone about the incident.

Over the past few decades, international concern and action have grown in regard to intimate partner violence against women, and various conferences have been held and resolutions and manifestos drafted in an effort to reduce its incidence (Baker, 2006). The first convention to declare discrimination against women as an international issue was the 1979 United Nations Convention on the Elimination of all Forms of Discrimination against Women. In 1994, the UN designated domestic violence as a human rights issue (Rodney, 1995). Conventions, however, do not have the same binding force as domestic law, although they place an externally monitored international standard of accountability upon signatory countries. United Nations conventions are also designed to raise awareness and have widened the terms of reference associated with domestic violence.

Most governments continue to express concern about all forms of domestic violence and abuse but the absence of public money remains the major impediment to establishing effective programs and services. Private donations as well as public funds support transition houses for battered women, and these safe houses are often staffed by volunteers and operate on the verge of closing due to lack of ongoing funds. Follow-up therapy and counselling may also be necessary for the entire family but these services also cost money to establish and maintain. Despite acknowledging the serious nature of this kind of violence, states have not always delivered sufficient program funding to deal with the rising number of reported cases. Nevertheless, many women manage to leave their abusive relationships and to care for themselves and their children alone, or find more satisfying relationships. However, a minority of 'disadvantaged' women do not find their subsequent relationships as fulfilling as they expected, as we will see in the next section.

Barriers to Legal Marriage

Policy discussion, especially in the United States, has often suggested that the plight of lone mothers living on low earnings or social benefits would be resolved if they simply married their male partners. Public campaigns have tried to convince low-income Americans of the value of marriage, and state income-support programs have been made less generous to encourage unmarried couples receiving social benefits to legalize their relationships. American research suggests that those with higher educational qualifications and incomes have much higher marriage rates than poorer and less-educated people. In contrast, the 'disadvantaged' are only half as likely to marry but more often cohabit. When disadvantaged people do marry, their divorce rates tend to be higher, and these rates have been rising in recent years (McLaughlin and Lichter, 1997).

Qualitative and quantitative studies have uncovered a number of barriers to legal marriage among disadvantaged Americans. Edin and Reed (2005) reviewed the recent research and found that disadvantaged men and women highly value marriage but are unable to meet the high standards of relationship quality and financial stability they believe are necessary to sustain a marriage and avoid divorce. Many see marriage as 'sacred', more committed than cohabitation, and something they want to do 'some day'. Many cohabiting partners with low income and low education are already parents and have had a child by another partner, although this child was not usually planned. Nearly one-third of poor American women aged 25 and older have had a child outside marriage compared to five per cent who were not poor (Hoffman and Foster, 1997).

American research suggests that low-income men and women do not view marriage as a prerequisite for child-bearing but they often say that children are better off when raised within marriage (Edin and Reed, 2005). However, the ideal of marriage remains unrealized because of the complexities of their lives. Their relationships are often conflict-ridden and involve partner violence and frequent separations. Furthermore, the stigma of divorce is deemed greater than the stigma of having a child outside marriage. Both men and women struggle to find employment that can pay the bills, and many couples experience bouts of unemployment and low-paid jobs. Before they can marry, many feel that they need a secure income, enough money for a mortgage on a modest home, some furniture, a car, some savings in the bank, and some money for a 'decent' wedding (Edin and Kefalas, 2005).

Over the past few decades, legal marriage seems to have lost some of its instrumental value as more women become self-supporting, contraception and abortion are widely available, premarital sex and cohabitation have become more socially acceptable, and marriage is no longer necessary for women's social or legal status (Edin and Reed, 2005). In fact, legal marriage would make little difference to the daily lives of many mothers and fathers who are already cohabiting. Yet American research has found that the symbolic value of marriage remains. Edin and Kefalas (2005) argued that marriage has become a symbol of status and luxury rather than of necessity. It has become a relationship that carries much higher expectations of relationship quality and financial stability, and many of the poor cannot meet this higher marital standard.

Conclusion

Although more people now cohabit without the blessing of religion or the legitimation of the state, the majority of people eventually marry and stay together for life. In both Western and Eastern countries, people marry for a variety of reasons, and many remain married even when their relationship is not particularly satisfying, either emotionally or sexually. Two can live cheaper than one, few parents want to forfeit the daily companionship of their children, marriage partners derive satisfaction and esteem from other aspects of their lives, and most married people want to grow old with their families intact.

Nevertheless, satisfaction seldom remains the same over the years of marriage, as children come and go and personal circumstances change. Levels of satisfaction tend to be the highest at the beginning of marriage as well as after many years of life together, but the middle years seem more prone to disappointments. Some of the problems in middle age are related to difficulties dealing with adolescent children, but even child-free couples report lower levels of satisfaction at this time. However, marital roles are changing as more mid-life women are employed full-time, while more men are able (or forced) to change jobs, return to school, or create their own businesses. Some of these transitions may strengthen levels of satisfaction but they may also push marriage partners towards separation.

Some couples who stay together into old age have always been satisfied with their marriages while others manage either to adapt to their disillusionment or to reinvigorate their relationship. Over time, most relationships are cemented with shared understandings, memories, children and grandchildren, and mutual love, caring, and companionship. Although social scientists tend to focus on conflict and marriage breakdown, most couples in reality remain together for life. Yet this is seldom reiterated in the media or in academic research.

Summary

This chapter shows that marriage remains the choice of lifestyle for most people, but that a growing portion of young people are choosing to live together before settling with a more permanent partner. However, the kind of relationship that young people choose tends to reflect their social-class backgrounds, culture, and educational and employment opportunities.

Questions for Critical Thought

1. Why do cohabiting couples who eventually marry so often include the symbols of traditional weddings (such as virginal white dresses, gold wedding rings, and fathers giving women to husbands)?

2. Why do women continue to live with men who abuse them? Why don't they leave when abusive incidents first occur?

3. Do young people still aspire to lifelong marriages or do these relationships now seem boring?

Suggested Readings ———————————————

Ambert, Anne-Marie. 2005. 'Same-Sex Couples and Same-Sex-Parent Families: Relationships, Parenting and Issues of Marriage', Vanier Institute of the Family, at: <www.vifamily.ca>. Ambert surveys the literature on same-sex relationships and discusses the relationship between sexual preference, commitment, and family practices.

Edin, Kathryn and Joanna M. Reed. 2005. 'Why Don't They Just Get Married? Barriers to Marriage among the Disadvantaged', *Marriage and Child Wellbeing* 15, 2: 117–36.

Wu, Zheng. 2000. *Cohabitation: An Alternative Form of Family Living*. Toronto: Oxford University Press. This book examines the implication of rising rates of cohabitation from academic and policy perspectives, using Canadian data.

Suggested Websites ———————————————

Australian Bureau of Statistics *www.abs.gov.au*
     This website contains a wealth of statistics and studies on families in Australia.

National Council on Family Relations *www. ncfr.org*
     This American association provides an educational forum for family researchers, educators, and practitioners to share in the development and dissemination of knowledge about families and relationships.

Chapter 4

Child-bearing, Child-rearing, and Childhood

Learning Objectives

- To understand how parenting, childhood, and adolescence have been influenced by changing patterns of education and work, greater use of technology, professional practices, and new ideas about childbirth, parenthood, and children's rights
- To acknowledge that socio-economic patterns are evident in fertility
- To learn how the state has supported children who are poor, abused, or neglected

Chapter Outline

This chapter discusses research about why people have children and why fertility rates have declined in Western countries. It also presents findings about the social history of childhood and parenting, the growing medicalization of childbirth, child welfare and care issues, and new patterns of parenting.

Introduction

In this chapter, I explore the ways that decisions and experiences relating to pregnancy and childbirth have changed over the decades and whether childhood in the twenty-first century is much different than it used to be. These questions can be approached by examining research and theories, as well as public controversies and media representations about having and raising children. Generally, the research suggests that having children has become more of a choice but that social patterns exist in who chooses to reproduce, and in the timing and experience of childbirth. Secondly, childbirth has come to be dominated by the medical profession and technological interventions. Thirdly, perceptions of childhood, parenting styles, and the life experiences of children and youth have varied over the decades with changes in the economic value of children to families, new ideas about child development, different forms of supervision, more influence from the media and technology, and broader changes in the larger society (Synnott, 1983; Wall, 2004, 2009).

Children's upbringing is increasingly influenced by television, videos, computer games, advertising, the Internet, other children, and non-family care providers, as well as by the care and supervision from parents, siblings, and other close relatives. In addition, educational expectations and opportunities have increased for all children but especially for those from lower-income families. Nevertheless, the research indicates that children's **socialization** and life chances continue to be influenced by their gender, their family circumstances, and the political and economic environment of their country of residence.

If we want to understand how societal changes have influenced child-bearing, child-rearing, and childhood, the central questions to be considered include how much change has actually occurred in recent decades and what factors continue to influence parenting and growing up in liberal welfare states today? Let us begin by examining studies of why people have children.

Why Have Children?

Although most adults produce children, they are now more likely to question whether or not they really want to, when they should start trying to conceive, and how many children they should have (VIF, 2008). In 2006, only seven per cent of Canadian women aged 20 to 39 reported that they did not want any children. On average, the number of children the others intend to have is 2.2 for women and 2.1 for men (ibid.). In Australia, only five per cent say that their ideal is to have no children (with more men than women saying this), and the ideal family size is slightly higher than in Canada (Weston et al., 2004). Interestingly, actual fertility rates are lower in Canada than Australia, more Canadian women work full-time, and the Canadian provinces provide lower levels of income support for mothers caring at home (Baker, 2006).

Raising children into well-adjusted, socially responsible adults is a difficult task requiring vision, commitment, and years of hard work. Nevertheless, researchers have found that most parents see children as the natural outcome of adulthood and marriage rather than a conscious choice. In attempting to explain why people continue to reproduce despite the well-publicized hardships of child-rearing, sociologists gloss over parental instincts or biological explanations and focus on two social reasons. One relates to social pressures while the other emphasizes costs and benefits.

Since the 1970s, sociologists have argued that having children is perceived as a sign of maturity, normality, and sexual competence. These conclusions are reached after questioning parents and studying people's reactions to childless couples. When parents are asked why they had children, they usually portray the experience in positive terms, discussing opportunities to relive the joys of childhood, to transmit their values and knowledge, and to receive unconditional love. They also mention desires to create their own social group, and to pass on their family name and genes (Cameron, 1990; May, 1995; Erfani and Beaujot, 2006). In contrast, individuals who choose *not* to reproduce or to bear only one child tend to be stigmatized by others (Morell, 1994; Cameron, 1990, 1997; Baker, 2005b). People who are childless by choice (or 'child-free') are often viewed as selfish, unloving, irresponsible, immature, materialistic, career-oriented, lonely, and even psychologically unstable. Younger people tend to view the childless choice more liberally, yet it is still widely accepted that married couples *should* produce children.

The social pressure to reproduce comes from many sources: religious leaders, government officials, family, friends, and even strangers. The churches have viewed the purpose of marriage as reproduction, and after the wedding ceremony friends and family often symbolize this expectation by throwing symbols of fertility (such as confetti or rice) on the couple. Governments and community leaders continue to see children as necessary because they will become the future generation of taxpayers, voters, workers, and consumers. Parents often want grandchildren to amuse them and later watch over them in old age, and siblings want nieces and nephews to expand their family networks. Parents expect to share their child-related experiences with friends, as well as stories about the joys and problems of child-rearing. Television advertisements, especially for cleaning products and fast food, show happy parents (usually mothers) interacting with healthy, smiling, and loving children. These images encourage us to see child-rearing as desirable and rewarding. Consequently, many people romanticize child-rearing and downplay the disadvantages.

Another theory about why people reproduce is that they believe children will enhance their lives in ways that compensate for the expense and hard work of child-rearing. Parents say they receive pleasure and a sense of achievement from watching their children develop, and that producing children enhances personal and sexual identity (Willen and Montgomery, 1996; Erfani and Beaujot, 2006). Cameron (1990) studied why New Zealanders reproduce and found that over half the respondents felt that companionship and the simple enjoyment of children were important reasons. 70 per cent also agreed that having children provided a sense of continuity after death. Women emphasized passing down knowledge about family history while men focused on having sons to carry on the family name and line (ibid., 42). New Zealand parents also said that having children reinforced adult status and identity, strengthened marital relationships, and made individuals 'complete' (Cameron, 1990: 60). Reproduction is associated with maturity because it provides visible evidence of sexual and social competence. It also serves as a rite of passage or transition from childhood to adulthood, and fulfills dominant conceptions of masculinity and femininity. The disadvantages of having children include the amount of time and cost involved in raising them, and the loss of personal freedom. Nevertheless, most people highlight the social and psychological rewards, and believe that parenthood is superior to a childless marriage.

Patterns in Childlessness

Social patterns are evident in who reproduces, with some people less likely to become parents. Differences are apparent by country but men are more likely than women to reproduce because they have a longer biological period of fecundity and more men re-partner with younger women after separation or widowhood (Dykstra, 2006). Historically, some eras produced more childlessness and, in many countries, women born around 1900 were less likely to have children than women born around 1950 (Rowland, 2007). Childlessness is also associated with 'late starts' in independent living, education, and marriage, as well as high education and stable employment for women (Hagestad and Call, 2007). Women with post-graduate education and professional or managerial jobs are less likely than comparable men to marry and have children (Beaujot, 2000), probably because women perceive that child-rearing slows their careers.

The distinction between voluntary and involuntary childlessness tends to be blurred by circumstances and constraints (Dykstra, 2006; Rowland, 2007; Tough et al., 2007). Circumstances leading to childlessness include war, (male) unemployment, financial insecurity, few opportunities to meet suitable partners, separation and divorce, and decisions made by partners. Individuals who make a conscious decision to remain childless tend to weigh the advantages and disadvantages and discuss the issues at length with their partner, family, or friends before finalizing their decision (Cameron, 1997; Gillespie, 2003). However, women who choose not to procreate have to account for their choices in ways that women who become mothers do not (Gillespie, 1999; Hird and Abshoff, 2000).

Infertility seem to be increasing in urban industrialized societies with higher levels of pollution, stressful lifestyles, sexually-transmitted diseases, higher rates of obesity, more substance abuse, and delayed attempts at conception with older marriages. Those experiencing fertility problems are encouraged to seek medical assistance, although the live birth rates from reproductive procedures are often low and the price of treatment high. The fact that some couples are willing to spend large sums of household money on medically assisted conception illustrates the continuing importance of having children in postmodern society (Baker, 2004c).

Box 4.1 Childlessness and Social Exclusion

In Baker's study of New Zealand couples who seek fertility treatment (Baker, 2004c, 2005b), most participants said that they took it for granted that they would reproduce when they became adults. A 29-year-old woman commented that she always assumed she would have children:

> When I was about thirteen, from that age, I started collecting things for my future children...things like baby clothes, baby toys, always only little stuff to go in the glory box [hope chest or trousseau]. . . . So it was always going to be my destiny at some stage.

A 34-year-old married businessman said:

> I never for one moment thought I would be without children... (I imagined) being married at 30, director of a company by the time I was 33 and financially I wanted to be in the position, by the time I was 35, to have children...so I had it kind of formally mapped out in my mind.

A number of participants reported that their inability to reproduce made them feel frustrated, worried about marital stability, and excluded from 'normal' adult life, especially when their siblings and friends were having children. For example, a 34-year-old wife said:

> I have a lot of guilt because I perceive it is my fault that we don't have any children...I have a lot of anxiety about (my husband) leaving me for somebody who can have children.

A 38-year-old husband commented:

> You definitely miss out on something [if you don't have children] because a lot of my friends have got kids...When we've gone out with couples who have got kids and we haven't and the couples with kids talk kids, we can't contribute....

(Continued)

One 38-year-old woman in a cohabiting relationship said:

We've had nine friends in the last two months who told us that they're pregnant and only four of those I think it was planned as such. So we've very quietly and privately struggled with that.... Deep down, we're saying 'What about us? What about us?'

Source: Baker (2005b: 521–43). Reprinted by permission of the publisher.

Declining Family Size

In recent decades, fertility rates have declined in many countries, as Table 4.1 indicates. Demographers estimate that if each couple produced about 2.1 children, population stability would be maintained and countries could replace their deaths with new births. However, the total fertility rates (or the average number of children per woman who has completed child-bearing) are now

Table 4.1   Total Fertility Rates in Selected Countries, 1970 and 2005–2006 (Births per woman)

Country	1970	2005–2006
Australia	2.9	1.8
Canada	2.0	1.5
Denmark	2.0	1.8
France	2.5	1.9
Germany	2.0	1.3
Italy	2.4	1.3
(South) Korea	3.0*	1.1
New Zealand	3.3	2.0
Spain	2.9	1.3
Sweden	1.9	1.8
United Kingdom	2.4	1.8
United States	2.0	2.0

*1976 figure

Sources: OECD (2005b: 29), based on data chart GE3.2. Decline in completed fertility and increase in mean age of mother at first childbirth; Gray, Qu, and Weston, 2007: 8.

below replacement levels in all OECD countries except in Mexico and Turkey (OECD, 2007: 44). In Canada, the total fertility rate was 1.5 in 2006, well below the replacement rate, but the fertility rate in South Korea has plummeted even further to 1.1 in 2006 (Gray et al., 2007). Even the Southern European countries now experience low fertility rates; both Italy and Spain had total fertility rates of 2.4 in 1970 but 1.3 in recent years (ibid.). The recent figures for Southern Europe obscure any previous statistical association between high fertility, Catholicism, and traditional family values (Castles, 2002).

Policy-makers are often concerned about declining fertility because it could lead to 'population aging' or a higher percentage of seniors in the population. This could signal future labour shortages, declining productivity, and insufficient taxpayers to finance the medical expenses and pensions of the higher proportion of seniors. Despite these concerns, fertility rates have been declining since the late 1800s, influenced by industrialization, urbanization, and the rising cost of child-rearing. Infant mortality rates began to decline in the 1920s with improved living standards and better health care, permitting couples to produce fewer children because more were expected to reach maturity (Chesnais, 1992). Child-rearing costs also increased, while the benefits of large families gradually declined in urban areas. The financial cost of having children is now calculated in terms of women's lost earnings, the need for more spacious accommodation in better school zones or safer areas, as well as the direct costs of children's food, clothing, care, and education.

Fertility rates have also declined because few parents now rely on their children for old age care as OECD countries provide old age security programs. In addition, children are required to attend school and cannot be asked to support the family. Declining fertility is also related to improvements in contraception, legalized abortion, preferences for smaller families, and the difficulty mothers experience combining employment with child-rearing (McDonald, 2000; Weston and Parker, 2002; Gray et al., 2007).

Women are now bearing their first child later in life, at an average age of 27.5 in OECD countries in 2004, compared to 24.0 in 1970, which reduces overall fertility rates (OECD, 2007: 45). The growing tendency to postpone pregnancy provides advantages for women, who can complete their education, find paid work, and possibly become eligible for parental benefits. However, postponing motherhood sometimes makes conception more difficult, pregnancy riskier, and contributes to lower national fertility. This suggests that lower fertility rates may be beneficial to women but be perceived as a problem for the nation.

Fertility rates are no longer related to women's employment rates as they were a few generations ago, and most women cannot afford or no longer wish to refrain from paid work in order to raise large families (Castles, 2002). Yet fertility rates are relatively high in countries such as France and Sweden, with formal care provisions for preschool children and flexible work arrangements for employed parents. Rates are also high in countries with a large percentage of cultural minorities who value reproduction but where birth control is less accessible, and unregulated child care is inexpensive, such as the United States. In contrast, women tend to have fewer children when they must struggle to earn a living, and public discourse makes them feel guilty about 'neglecting' their children.

Births outside marriage have also increased but most are to cohabiting couples in which the woman is between 25 and 35 years old. In the Nordic countries, over half of all births now occur outside marriage compared to about 10 per cent in 1960, while about 45 per cent of births in New Zealand, 32 per cent in Australia, and 28 per cent in Canada occurred outside marriage in 2004 (OECD, 2007a). Teenage birth rates have also declined, from an average of 34 births per 1,000 women aged 15–19 in 1980 to 16 in 2004 in OECD countries (OECD, 2005b: 86, 2007a). However, there are many country variations. The teen birth rate in Canada was 13.8 in 2004 but 50.3 in the United States, compared to a high of 67.3 in Mexico and a low of 3.5 in Korea (OECD, 2007a), suggesting that cultural, socio-economic, and social service factors influence these rates. The declining teenage pregnancy rate is usually applauded because early pregnancy is associated with disadvantage, including low education, poor earning capacity, and poor life chances for children and mothers (Hobcraft and Kiernan, 2001).

Cross-national variations in teenage birth rates are influenced by trends in sexuality, access to contraception, ideas about women's roles, and the percentage of disadvantaged groups in the population (OECD, 2005b: 86). Teen fertility rates remain relatively high in countries such as the United States with large percentages of visible minorities with low household incomes, few employment opportunities, and lack of access to contraception. These minorities tend to cohabit and marry at younger ages and to place a higher value on parenthood as an indicator of adult status and love between partners (Mink, 1998; Edin and Reed, 2005).

National fertility rates also vary by parents' economic circumstances (OECD, 2008: 63). The current stereotype is that poor people make more babies but this is not the case in many European countries that provide generous benefits for families with children. For example, in countries such as Austria, Denmark, France, Germany, and Sweden, the top income quintile (or one-fifth) of income-earners have more children than the bottom quintile. However, in the liberal states, the poor are more likely to reproduce (ibid.). Women with high levels of education and strong commitment to career are less likely than other women to marry and have children (Weedon et al., 2006).

In the 1960s, the United Nations began to encourage governments to support 'zero population growth' and to provide reproductive services such as legalized abortion and contraception. Now, as fertility rates drop farther than anticipated, more OECD countries are expressing concern about the national economic consequences of declining fertility. Researchers and policy-makers generally agree that lower teenage birth rates are socially beneficial but they do not always acknowledge the advantages for other women. In families with many children, wives are less likely to be employed but the family is more likely to require state income supplements. Having fewer children enables women to pursue their educational goals and retain employment, which raises the family's living standards and provides tax revenue for the state. Fewer children per family could also enable each child to receive more parental attention. Although developing countries attempt to counteract overpopulation and urban crowding by promoting family planning, OECD countries often fund these services only for low-income or 'problem' families, urging wealthier couples to reproduce. This suggests that having children is not always seen as women's choice or the couple's decision but as something governments want to control.

In the next section, I examine some historical changes in the social circumstances of child-rearing as well as attitudes about parenting and childhood.

Parenting and Childhood in the Past

In the nineteenth century, parenting experiences differed considerably by gender, age, social class, and culture, just as they do today. However, they were particularly influenced by unreliable contraception, the assumption of heterosexuality, and gendered marital roles. Marriage often implied that the wife was sexually available to her husband on a regular basis, but unless couples used some form of contraception or abstained from sexual intercourse many wives spent a considerable amount of time during their pre-menopausal years in pregnancy, lactation, and miscarriage. Contraception has been available for hundreds of years but in the past it was less reliable, difficult to purchase, and socially unacceptable to use. The common view was that child-bearing and rearing should be sufficient vocation for women, although a few women could afford to develop larger spheres of influence. Nevertheless, using contraception and remaining childless were interpreted by some as a rejection of femininity, religious values, and traditional marriage.

Both men and women were expected to marry and reproduce. Those who did not want children often avoided marriage, but single adults were continually pressured to find a partner and 'start a family' unless they joined a religious order that promoted celibacy or were ill or disabled. Women's employment options were limited and single women were often expected to care for their aging parents or sibling's children; many lived with relatives with little autonomy or status, instead of developing independent lives. In rural districts, some sons remained on the family farm to assist their fathers and therefore found fewer opportunities to meet potential wives. When men did marry, they had to be prepared to support a wife and new baby within the first year of marriage.

Husbands were expected to continue the family line, represent the family to the community, earn the household income, and become the main disciplinarian over vaginal births, as an abdominal scar is seen as a lesser disadvantage than a 'loose vagina' from vaginal birth that may impede sexual satisfaction. This has led to media articles about women who are 'too posh to push' (Asthana, 2005). However, elective Caesareans not only are more costly than vaginal births but also require longer recovery time (Tew, 1998). For these reasons, elective Caesareans remain options for wealthier patients whose doctors are willing to accommodate them.

The steadily increasing rate of Caesarean births has become one of the most contested issues in maternity care (Walker et al., 2002). The World Health Organization (WHO) has stated that Caesareans should be performed only with medical justification, suggesting that the optimum rate should fall between five and 15 per cent of births (WHO, 1998: 77). However, few countries have rates within these levels and in some jurisdictions, Caesarean rates range from 25–45 per cent of all births (Walker et al., 2002: 28). Doctors are more likely than mid- wives to rely on technological interventions and drugs, which means that the clients of midwives require less postpartum care and recovery time, and their services are less costly to public health-care systems (Tew, 1998; Monari et al., 2008). However, comparing hospital births to home births by midwives gives a false impression of the consequences of each option. Higher-risk maternity cases are generally accepted by obstetricians rather than midwives and riskier births usually take place in hospitals, which raises the neonatal mortality rates of hospital births delivered by obstetricians compared to home births attended by midwives.

If doctors caution pregnant women that a vaginal birth could be risky, few patients could independently evaluate this advice. Neither doctors nor preg- nant women and their families want to take unnecessary risks in childbirth but the medical profession remains powerful enough in many liberal states to be able to pressure governments to accept their practices and limit the powers of midwives. The fact that Caesareans are more often performed on wealthier women suggests that doctors may have chosen to benefit financially from these operations without the necessary medical grounds for the procedures (Walker et al., 2002; Ford et al., 2003).

The **medicalization**, bureaucratization, and privatization of childbirth ser- vices have concerned many patients and their families, but have also forced health officials and hospital administrators to improve public birthing facili- ties. Private hospitals and birthing centres offer more luxuries to patients who can afford them; however, cost-cutting measures are widespread in both private and public institutions. In the 1940s and 1950s, women could expect a two- week 'confinement', but now they are expected to give birth and leave the hos- pital within a few days. This short stay may be justified for health reasons but it has also served as a cost-cutting measure (Tew, 1998).

Health-care services are being regionalized in some countries and responsi- bility is being shifted from public institutions to informal networks and unpaid caregivers (Armstrong et al., 2002). Benoit et al. (2002) argued that non-urban women in British Columbia view the regionalization of maternity-care services in a largely negative light. They complain about the lack of choice in care providers, discontinuous care, and inadequate quality of care. However, many politicians believe that it is more important to reduce the cost of public health care, especially as more services will be needed in the future as the population grows older. Yet the rising cost of childbirth is only one concern. As more mothers are employed, they and their partners worry about losing the wife's income during childbirth and recovery.

The International Labour Organization (ILO) Maternity Protection Convention of 2000 states that pregnant women should be entitled to at least 14 weeks of paid leave from work and that when they return they should be entitled to a daily reduction of working hours with full remuneration for breast-feeding (ILO, 2000). The World Health Organization encourages new mothers to breast-feed because it is associated with numerous health benefits, including providing optimum nutrition for infants, reducing infectious diseases, and lowering infant mortality (WHO and UNICEF, 1990). However, middle-class women are more likely to breast-feed than low-income women. For employed mothers, the duration of breast-feeding may be influenced by job control, employment security, leave provisions, and breast-feeding facilities.

Paid leave at childbirth or adoption can be gender-specific or gender-neutral. Maternity benefits are gender-specific and focus on maternal and child health and women's employment equity. Parental benefits are gender-neutral and have been used as an inducement for couples to reproduce and for men to become more involved in infant care. Both have been seen also as citizenship rights for employees. Comparative research suggests that the model chosen depends on political lobbying within the jurisdiction and the ideology of the party in power (Heitlinger, 1993; Gauthier, 1996; Hantrais, 2004). Political pressure may be national and come from women's groups or men's rights groups, or it can originate from supranational organizations, such as the ILO, that encourage member states to develop minimum standards (Hantrais, 2000). However, the type of leave and benefit provisions fit in with existing social programs, political priorities, and current views of citizenship rights (Baker, 2006).

Medically Assisted Conception

Fertility problems seem to be increasing in industrialized countries but they might simply be reported more often now that couples can obtain medical assistance. Those experiencing problems can use the Internet to find information about the procedures offered by fertility clinics, the probability of success, potential risks, and personal costs. In countries with private clinics, patients with adequate resources can purchase the services they believe will help them,

Most adults who are abused as children do *not* become child abusers, although various factors accumulate to augment the risk. Parents who abuse alcohol and drugs, and who live in impoverished and violent homes, are more likely to maltreat their children. Maltreatment contributes to children's depression, anxiety, and hostility, as well as to certain types of behaviour such as physical inactivity, smoking, alcoholism, drug abuse, risky sexual practices, and suicide (UNICEF, 2003: 19). Lack of affordable housing encourages women and children to stay in abusive homes and creates overcrowded conditions that heighten family tensions and promote contagious and chronic diseases.

Children are also negatively affected by witnessing violence in the home. Each year about 12 per cent of North American women experience intimate-partner violence and 10 million children witness this violence (Graham-Bermann and Edleson, 2001: 3). In New Zealand, six per cent of children witnessed 'adults hurting other adults' in the home, while 16 per cent witnessed adults hurting children (MSD, 2008). Many mothers who experience domestic violence fear for their children's safety but this fear is sometimes minimized by complex and often hostile court systems (Jaffe et al., 2003: 17). A shift in awareness towards recognizing the effects of domestic violence on children has been precipitated by research and international conferences (Krug et al., 2002: 103). Consequently, many countries have amended child custody policies to take into account the parents' history of domestic violence. There is clear evidence of growing concern about the cost of violent behaviour to individuals, families, employers, and taxpayers.

Indigenous and minority group children have been over-represented in the caseloads of child welfare systems in the liberal states (Baker, 2006). The former practices of keeping indigenous children in state-regulated residential schools or encouraging adoption by white families have fallen into disrepute. Many of these children suffered from cultural confusion and reported some form of abuse after living with white foster families or in residential schools. Kin care is now viewed as less contentious because it keeps children within their local community and cultural group. Consequently, considerable effort has gone into trying to apply foster care processes and standards to kinship care. Even though research comparing child well-being in kin care with foster care is underdeveloped and sometimes contradictory, governments continue to encourage these practices (Connolly, 2003).

'Disadvantaged' children are identified by a number of 'risk factors', including growing up with persistent poverty and parental unemployment, with parents who have low education or are involved in substance abuse, mental illness, or depression. Risk factors also include living in families that are struggling to be integrated into the prevailing language or culture. Childcare researchers and child welfare experts argue that these disadvantaged children can benefit most from early childhood services, in order to counteract significant inequalities of opportunity (UNICEF, 2008: 9). However, the children of employed parents also require childcare services.

Child Care Subsidies

Many countries subsidize child-care costs, especially for employed parents with low incomes. Some governments focus on not-for-profit centres or licensed homes (Jenson and Sineau, 2001b) but the liberal welfare states have also been funding for-profit care, including franchised services since the 1990s (Brennan, 2007a, 2007b). This is particularly a problem if the main care provider is in financial trouble and threatens to close, as was the case with ABC Learning Centres in Australia in 2008 (Kruger et al., 2008).

Governments could subsidize child-care generously for all parents (as in Sweden, France, and Quebec), or they could target meagre subsidies to low-income employed parents, as in many American states. In countries such as New Zealand, two-parent families requiring child-care used to pay the full cost if they had average incomes, but in 2007 the government introduced 20 hours a week of 'free' child-care for children attending early childhood education centres (although it does not always cover the full cost). The Australian government provides a tax rebate for low-income parents using child-care services but the cost is relatively high for middle-income parents. The Canadian government provides relatively generous tax breaks to cover the child-care expenses of employed parents, but the official receipts required are sometimes difficult to obtain from informal carers. Provincial governments in Canada subsidize child care for low-income families (Friendly and Beach, 2005).

Even when governments subsidize child care, the subsidy level can vary from a fraction of the fees to most of the cost. If governments see preschool care mainly as early childhood education, they may subsidize only a few hours a week. If they want to encourage maternal employment, they may subsidize care that covers the entire work week. Subsidized spaces usually are regulated by government, but the regulations can be minimal, covering mainly physical facilities, or they can be extensive, also covering the educational program and carer qualifications.

Whatever arrangement is favoured by the state, the number of children requiring care usually outstrips the availability of spaces in highly recommended centres. The shortage of regulated spaces means that most employed parents with preschool children are forced to rely on unregulated care or sitters in the liberal states (Baker, 2006). Caring for children is a challenging job yet generally pays the minimum wage or less, which means that child-care centres often experience difficulty attracting and retaining trained staff.

Most governments want to ensure that children are cared for by qualified providers in safe and stimulating environments but they are not always prepared to fund it. The provision of high-quality care is expensive, especially for infants, and costs rise when governments require professional qualifications for providers, educational programs, and nourishing food for children, and safe and congenial facilities. When the entire costs are passed on to parents, most

Table 4.2   Child-care Costs as Percentage of Net Income for Working Couples and Lone Parents

Country	2-earner families (both with average wages and 2 children)	2-earner families (1 with average wage, 1 with low wage and 2 children)	Lone parent (1 average wage and 2 children)
Australia	22	19	17
Canada	18	29	27
Denmark	9	10	9
France	18	17	15
New Zealand	21	26	42
Sweden	6	7	5
United Kingdom	26	27	9
United States	19	23	38
OECD Average	15	17	17

Source: Figures extracted from OECD (2007b: 59).

cannot afford this kind of care. Consequently, both government and employers sometimes subsidize child care, but they also want to ensure that the costs are manageable. France, Sweden, and Belgium have chosen to provide high-quality, government-regulated child care, but few English-speaking countries offer the same level of services (Brennan, 1998, 2007a; Jenson and Sineau, 2001a). The liberal states tend to keep social spending low and rely on parents to pay most child-care costs. Table 4.2 shows 2005 child-care costs as a percentage of household earnings for two-earner and sole-parent families in selected OECD countries, showing that the cost can be relatively high in the liberal states, except for sole parents in the United Kingdom.

The Extension of Adolescence

Parents usually grant more autonomy to adolescents than younger children, allowing teenagers more privileges and choices in their daily life and involving them in family decisions. Many parents encourage their adolescents to develop adult skills and eventually to expect to marry and establish their own households. This involves encouragement to become educated, develop job experience, interpersonal skills, and develop good judgment about relationships. Social historians and sociologists have investigated historical transitions in the life cycle and noted that adolescence has been prolonged in Western societies as young people remain in school longer and more of them depend on their parents for accommodation, meals, and financial assistance. Recent Canadian census figures show that 26 per cent of 25–29 year olds lived in the parental home in 2006 compared to only 15.6 per cent in 1986 (Statistics Canada, 2007c). Canadian young people who leave home earlier than their cohort tend to come from separated/divorced parents, larger families, to be less religious, and grow up in small towns (Beaupré et al., 2006).

Adolescents and young people have to deal with physiological and emotional changes, educational choices, relations with friends, new dating experiences, and imminent occupational decisions. They tend to be caught between childhood and adulthood, and sometimes feel that social expectations are unrealistic. While many are physically mature, they have not completed their education or secured full-time work, and therefore find it financially difficult to leave home. They may resent parental restrictions, feel that their parents are unreasonable and old-fashioned, and yearn for independence.

As children mature, they are confronted by media representations and advertisements for consumer goods that encourage them to aspire to material wealth, fashionable clothing, international travel, and personal fame. Many students feel compelled to work part-time to afford this kind of lifestyle but paid work may interfere with their studies. Gaining job experience and acquiring spending money may prove useful but many of the available jobs are low-level service positions with low wages. Although more adolescents and young adults now work part-time while they are students, fewer parents require them to pay 'room and board'. Young people may be expected to pay for some of their educational expenses, clothes, and leisure activities but many parents continue to pay for their accommodation and daily living expenses.

Adolescence is often a time of questioning about family history and parents' earlier activities and relationships. More young people now live with only one parent or in stepfamilies, and they may want to know details of their parents' past, including reasons for their marriage breakdown. About one per cent of babies are born from assisted conception, including sperm donations or donated eggs (Ford et al., 2003), but this percentage is expected to rise in the future. Undoubtedly, these young people will want to know something about their backgrounds and may press their parents for answers. As children grow older, they tend to question parental authority and want to establish the superiority of their own ideas and knowledge. Despite these conflicts, most parents derive considerable satisfaction from seeing their children grow into thinking individuals and watching them blossom into physical maturity.

Older people often think of adolescence as a time of hope, anticipation, and preparation for the future but some young people are depressed by their parents' relationship, their poor socio-economic circumstances, world events, and suggests that the expectations of parenting and typical parenting experiences have changed over the past few decades, causing additional stress for all parents but especially for those with low incomes who live in dangerous neighbour-hoods. In the next chapter, issues of employment and family money are examined in more detail.

Summary

The desire to have children and actual patterns of reproduction are influenced by early family experiences but also by opportunities and constraints in the larger society, such as access to contraception, the need to find paid work, and the cost of raising children. In addition, the experience of childbearing has been transformed by new attitudes and technologies, while childhood has been altered by more non-parental care, increasing consumerism, new communication technologies, and the need for prolonged education among youth.

Questions for Critical Thought

1. Are women who have elective Caesareans really 'too posh to push'?

2. Should the grandparents or extended families become the carers of children who are abused or neglected by their parents, or does this just perpetuate the problems?

3. Are parents neglecting their preschoolers by placing them in daycare centres while they work?

Suggested Readings

Doucet, Andrea. 2006. *Do Men Mother?* Toronto: University of Toronto Press. Based on narratives of Canadian fathers who are primary caregivers of children, this book explores the interplay between fathering and public policy, gender ideologies, social networks, and work-family policies.

Fox, Bonnie. 2001. 'The Formative Years: How Parenthood Creates Gender', *Canadian Review of Sociology and Anthropology* 38, 4: 373–90. This article is based on the author's study of heterosexual couples as they make the transition to parenthood. It illustrates the way particular versions of mothering and fathering are negotiated.

Wall, Glenda. 2009. 'Childhood and Child Rearing', in M. Baker, ed., *Families: Changing Trends in Canada*, 6th edn. Toronto: McGraw-Hill Ryerson, 91–107. This chapter focuses on the social construction of childhood through an examination of child-rearing advice, structural realities, and social policies relating to children.

Suggested Websites

Childcare Resource and Research Unit *www.childcarecanada.org*
The Childcare Resource and Research Unit (CRRU) focuses on early childhood education and child care (ECEC) and family policy both in Canada and internationally.

Centre for Families, Work, and Well-Being *www.worklifecanada.ca*
This University of Guelph centre provides information about child-care research projects.

day. Analysts then make statistical comparisons between various categories of participants, such as men and women; mothers, fathers, and childless couples; cohabiting, married, and single people; the young and old; and those working full-time and part-time. The fact that husbands and wives perform different household tasks is not necessarily a problem but in recent years most wives have increased their hours of paid work. Time-budget studies can tell us whether or not men do more housework when their wives increase their paid work, and if younger couples create a different sort of division of labour than older couples.

All the governments of the liberal welfare states produce official statistics on unpaid and paid work and some have been carrying out this research long enough to draw conclusions about changes over time. In brief, the studies of unpaid work tend to find that parents do more housework than non-parents, mothers more than fathers, married women more than cohabiting women, older women more than younger women, and women working part-time more than those working full-time. The Australian Bureau of Statistics has completed extensive time-budget surveys since the 1970s and has found that women perform about 70 per cent of unpaid domestic work, and this percentage is largely unaffected by their increasing employment rates. No matter how many hours of paid work an Australian wife does, her husband's contribution remains relatively constant (Bittman, 1991, 1995; Baxter, 1994; Baxter et al., 2008). Despite the increasing use of dishwashers, microwaves, automatic washers, and clothes dryers, Australians in the twenty-first century spend about the same amount of time in the kitchen and laundry as they did in 1974, partly because standards of cleanliness, cooking, and child care have been raised.

From the 1970s and 1980s, Australian women lost one hour of leisure time per day because they were working more for pay but they generally retained responsibility for domestic duties. By 1991, men were doing more work in the kitchen and laundry but many of these men were single, reflecting higher separation and divorce rates and older ages of marriage. Furthermore, two-thirds of men's unpaid work was done outdoors and many of the tasks were occasional ones rather than daily chores (Bittman, 1991). Using the 1997 Australian Time Use Survey, Bittman and Rice (1999) continued to show that husbands had *not* taken up the slack even though wives have increased their hours of paid work. Instead, 'domestic outsourcing' or the purchase of market substitutes for domestic labour helped Australian women resolve the time pressure created by an increasing commitment to paid work.

Canadian studies of unpaid work have found that women still do more domestic work than men although men's time on housework has increased slightly from 1986 to 2005 (Lindsay, 2008). The increase in male housework can be largely explained by the fact that more men are living outside nuclear family units or apart from their mothers and wives. In many countries, wives who are employed full-time tend to perform less housework than those who work part-time or are outside the **labour force**. Wives employed full-time either lower their housework standards, encourage other family members to share the work, or hire someone to clean their houses or care for their children. Having a larger number of children clearly represents more work for mothers. Yet, many women continue to retain all or most of the responsibility for indoor housework and child-rearing tasks, including the hiring and supervision of cleaners, care providers, and other family members (Ranson, 2009). Women with less than high school graduation and older women are more likely to accept sole responsibility for housework (Marshall, 1993, 1994). In addition to doing more housework, more women than men report that they organize and supervise household work, and that they engage in 'multi-tasking', which is to say that they complete several tasks at the same time (Eichler et al., forthcoming). The Canadian research suggests generational and social class differences in patterns of housework, as well as gender differences.

Gazso-Windle and McMullin (2003) used Canadian social survey data to explore the relationships among time availability, relative income, gender ideology, and the time spent on housework. They concluded that there is some evidence that partners, but especially husbands, 'trade off' the time they spend in housework by doing more paid work. However, women and men with higher incomes and education spend less time on housework and more time on child care. Ironically, wives spend *more* time on housework when their wages are higher or closer to their husband's, which suggests that being a successful family earner means something different for men and women. Some women may feel that they have to compensate for their success in the (male) breadwinning role by performing extra domestic tasks. Alternatively, the husbands of high-earning women may resent their 'intrusion' into family breadwinning and consequently may resist sharing domestic work. These researchers concluded that egalitarian notions about gender behaviour are more likely to influence Canadian men's participation in child care than in housework.

Box 5.1 shows some of the verbatim comments about who does the housework from a study of male and female academics with doctorates and permanent university positions, who I interviewed in New Zealand in 2008. These interviews suggested that the domestic division of labour was a source of conflict in many households.

Researchers from many countries have confirmed that mothers rather than fathers accept most of the responsibility for caring work even when they work full-time (Bittman and Pixley, 1997; Potuchek, 1997; Craig, 2006; Kitterød and Pettersen, 2006; Edlund, 2007; Craig and Bittman, 2008). Cross-national studies also show that housework and gender inequality in European countries are influenced by the level of technological development, religious culture, and individual religious beliefs (Voicu et al., 2008). Australian research found that women with university education tend to work longer hours for pay than other women but also that both men and women with university degrees spend more time with their children than less educated people do (Craig, 2006). In

Access to income clearly influences opportunities to own a home, enjoy comfortable accommodation, and accumulate family wealth. In recent years, researchers have compared rates of **child poverty** and used them as an indicator of the relative generosity of parental wages and social benefits for families in each country. The United Nations Children's Fund and the OECD regularly publish comparative statistics on the percentage of children living in households with 'low' incomes, usually defined as less than 50 per cent of the median income in that country, after taxes and government transfers and adjusted for family size. These figures show that poverty rates tend to be high in the liberal welfare states, such as the United States, Canada, and New Zealand, and much lower in the social democratic countries, such as Denmark, Finland, and Sweden (OECD, 2008a). However, poverty rates are much higher when children live only with their mother.

Since the 1960s, social researchers have also explored the connection between who earns household money and decisions about how it is spent. They concluded that the social meaning of money is important because who brings it into the household and how it is distributed relate to ideologies of gender and marriage (Pahl, 1995). Since the beginning of wage labour, husbands have been the primary earners in most households with European origins. The ideal of the **family wage** spread until, by the early 1900s, it meant that married men were paid a higher wage than single men or women. This wage was supposed to be sufficient to permit male breadwinners to support themselves, a wife, and two or three dependent children. As this employment practice was implemented, wives' earnings became viewed as less significant, as supplementary income for extras, and essentially disposable, regardless of how much they earned (Zelizer, 1994).

Although husbands earned most 'family money' in the past, they did not always manage it on their own. Often they kept some for themselves but gave the rest to their wives, who then purchased the necessities for the entire household. Sometimes husbands and wives managed their money jointly. When husbands managed their earnings themselves, they usually gave their wives a set amount of 'housekeeping money'. If wives earned their own money, they often used it to buy food or clothing for the children or to purchase household items; but some wives saw their personal earnings as their own money and kept it separate from household money. Current research suggests that the idea of the **male breadwinner** continues today even though most wives are also earners (Pahl, 2005).

The organization of family money is not always consciously discussed or decided but is influenced instead by cultural factors, by gender ideologies, and especially by the relative earnings of husbands and wives. Money is not the only valued resource in the **family economy**, nor is it equally valued in all households. Studying money allocation patterns reveals important cultural differences in access and control over family resources. For example, Fleming's

New Zealand research (1997) concluded that Maori and Pacific Island couples often lived within a wider family group where the use of their earnings could be dictated by the extended family. For couples with European origins, control over money is related to the relative amount earned by each partner and is more influenced by the notion that the husband should be the provider. In Maori and Pacific Island families, the provider role was not necessarily associated with power or authority, as other sources of male authority were available. Fleming (1999) also found that money allocation patterns in stepfamilies differed from first marriages, particularly with regard to supporting the other partner's children.

Although most wives are now employed, husbands typically earn considerably more than their wives. In British research, most married men and women defined their personal earnings as 'family money' but husbands were more likely than their wives to express this view (Pahl, 1995). Although there are several different ways of managing money, most couples pool their resources, and this money could be managed jointly, by the wife, or by the husband. Increased female employment is associated with the greater pooling of earnings that are managed jointly. In fact, the higher women's earnings are relative to their husbands, the more say wives have in how their combined earnings are spent (Vogler and Pahl, 1994). This suggests that longer hours of paid employment have enhanced wives' control over family money.

Despite more dual-earner families, few couples keep their earnings in separate bank accounts; however, this pattern is becoming more prevalent. In the 1990s, research found that only about three per cent of British couples kept all of their earnings separate but more recent research suggests that over a quarter of young British couples manage most of their earnings separately and combine only some that is designated for household expenses (Pahl, 2005). Independent money management was particularly characteristic of younger couples, those without children, and those where the woman was in full-time paid employment. Cohabitation, rather than legal marriage, also influences patterns of family money. New Zealand and British studies have found that women who cohabit are more likely than legally married women to have their own earnings and to keep their money separate from their partner's in order to maintain their independence (Elizabeth, 2001; Pahl, 2001).

Spending patterns also differ by gender. Canadian and British research suggests that wives and mothers tend to be responsible for buying food for the household, clothing for themselves and their children, and child care and school expenses. Men/fathers spent more of their earnings on meals out, alcohol, motor vehicles, repairs to the house, and gambling. Responsibility for other items of spending was more evenly distributed (Phipps and Burton, 1992; Ermisch, 2003; Pahl, 2005). With gendered differences in income, women often can raise their living standards by sharing a residence with an employed man, especially if they pool their earnings. However, if they keep their money separate and men work on short-term contracts, work part-time, or are self-employed. From the 1970s to the 1990s, many men were able to retire before the age of 65 with improvements to pension plans and increased savings from higher wages and interest rates (Myles, 1996). However, male wages from the 1970s to the 1990s did not always keep pace with rising living costs, and successive waves of men are now earning less than their elders at every stage in their work lives (Beaudry and Green, 1997). Consequently, the age of retirement for men is once again rising.

Although the husband still is the major breadwinner in most families, women's increased working hours and earnings are beginning to alter their expectations about marriage, children, and the household division of labour. Women's employment has increased dramatically in many countries, especially among mothers with children under six years of age (OECD, 2005b), as work patterns have been influenced by economic, ideological, and technological changes. First, the **service sector** of many national economies has expanded since the 1950s and 1960s, creating more clerical and service positions in education, retail sales, hospitality industries, health care, and the growing government bureaucracies. Many of these new jobs were thought to be appropriate for women because they were clean and safe and performed indoors. Some were also part-time, allowing mothers to retain most of their domestic and caring duties.

Women's employment also increased because families needed wives' wages to counteract the spiralling cost of living after the 1960s, especially where men's real wages were declining relative to living expenses in countries such as Canada and the United States (Torjman and Battle, 1999). Throughout the 1970s and 1980s, unemployment rates also increased and more families needed additional income to pay household bills. This included the consumer products that advertising campaigns induced people to buy, such as two cars and modern household appliances, as well as longer periods of formal education for the children. Furthermore, a shortage of employment opportunities encouraged more young people to stay in school, often while continuing to live in the parental home, which increased financial pressure on the entire family (Kobayashi, 2007).

The third reason for rising employment rates among women was that feminist ideologies, revived in the 1960 and 1970s, encouraged them to continue their schooling and use their education to contribute directly to household earnings and the larger society. North American feminists in particular argued that women should gain financial independence from their fathers and husbands in order to achieve equality with men, to realize their potential, and to establish an autonomous household if they so wished (Friedan, 1963; Pierson et al., 1993). At the same time, feminists in Britain, Australia, and New Zealand focused more on gaining government support for mothering at home, portraying women as different from men in their life goals and personal experiences (Land, 1980; Baker and Tippin, 1999). More North American women chose to find paid work in order to use their education, further their ambitions, earn their own money, raise their bargaining power in marriage, and contribute to household purchases and public life.

Fourth, more effective contraception permitted women to better control their pregnancies, especially after the contraceptive pill was marketed in the mid-1960s. Effective contraception enabled women to continue their education and work outside the home throughout their fertile years. Widespread use of contraception also meant that fewer employers worried about unexpected pregnancy among their female staff and were therefore willing to hire and promote women workers. Generally, modern contraceptives have enabled women to acquire higher education, reduce their fertility, and plan for a lifetime of paid work, if they so choose.

Despite these changes, women's employment rates remain much lower than men's in OECD countries, where 80.5 per cent of men compared to 61.1 per cent of women were employed in 2007 (OECD, 2008b: 337/8). Some gender convergence is apparent in the type of jobs and the hours of work, but men and women continue to perform different kinds of work and men are more likely to work full-time, overtime, and in positions of responsibility. Women are far more likely than men to accept part-time employment in all OECD countries, as Table 5.1 indicates (OECD, 2008b), and part-time work is less likely to lead to seniority or higher lifetime wages. Instead, it creates short-term solutions and long-term problems for women. Table 5.1 also shows that women tend to earn considerably less than men, especially in Japan but also in North America, Germany, the United Kingdom, and Canada, and that the incidence of low-paid

Table 5.1   Labour Force Characteristics in Selected Countries, 2006–07

Country	Women's Share of Part-Time Employment	% Gender Wage Gap*	Incidence of Low Pay (%)**
Australia	71.6	15	16.0
Canada	68.0	21	22.0
Denmark	62.8	9	12.0
France	80.3	12	-
New Zealand	72.6	7	12.9
Sweden	65.0	15	6.4
United Kingdom	77.4	21	20.5
United States	68.4	20	24.5
OECD average	72.8	18	16.8

* the difference between the median earnings of men and women, relative to men's earnings.

** the percentage of workers earning less than 2/3 of the median earnings.

Source: From OECD, 2008b, *OECD Employment Outlook*, pp. 352, 358, and OECD, 2009, *OECD Employment Outlook*, pp. 274.

child-care program that required parents to pay only $5 per day for care, whether or not parents were in paid work. The Quebec government also increased the number of spaces, the wages of educators, and its child-care budget at a time when neighbouring provinces were making cuts. However, in 2003 the Parti Québécois lost the election to the Liberals, who soon announced that they intended to slow the expansion of the child-care program, increase parental fees, and encourage for-profit child care (CRRU, 2003). However, public support for these subsidies remained high, although the cost was raised to $7 per day.

Countries vary in the focus and level of childcare subsidies; some focus on lone-parent households while others provide subsidies for low-income households, as we saw in Chapter 4. However, most countries also urge low-income mothers to enter paid work. Paid childbirth leave and affordable child care are necessary for women's employment equity, but these programs alone will not resolve the gender-based inequalities in work. The structure of paid work needs to be altered to remove the assumption that it is separate from personal life. The design of leave programs must acknowledge that women's feelings of obligation to children and partners have encouraged them to accept part-time or temporary employment, limit overtime work, take unpaid leave, relocate with their partner's occupation, and accept lower wages. Therefore, social programs need to focus on providing affordable and accessible child care, improving pay equity, raising girls' interest in occupational achievement, and increasing the participation of both boys and men in child care and housework. However, reforms that cost public or employer dollars are less likely to occur under neo-liberal restructuring or in economic hard times.

The resources that governments spend on families (including child payments and allowances, parental leave, and child-care support) vary considerably by country, as Table 5.5 indicates. In addition, the areas of support vary; they

Table 5.5   Social Spending on Families* as Percentage of Gross Domestic Product, 2003

Country	Cash	Services	Family-related Tax Breaks	Total
Australia	2.6	0.7	0.0	3.4
Canada	0.9	0.2	0.1	1.2
Denmark	1.6	2.3	0.0	3.9
France	1.4	1.6	0.8	3.8
New Zealand	1.9	0.4	0.0	2.3
Sweden	1.6	1.9	0.0	3.5
United Kingdom	2.2	0.8	0.4	3.3
United States	0.1	0.6	0.7	1.4
OECD Average	1.3	0.9	0.2	2.4

* includes child payments and allowances, parental leave benefits, and child care support.

Source: Figures extracted from OECD (2007a: Chart 4.1).

may invest more in cash benefits but less in social services. In this table, Canada and the United States look particularly ungenerous compared to Denmark and France.

Conclusion: The Growing Impact of Paid Work on Family Life

Throughout much of the twentieth century, married men were the main family earners while married women cared for the home and children. Women usually worked in the formal labour force before marriage but not always afterwards, working fewer hours than men, earning lower wages, and more often earning money at home. Today, most women are employed regardless of their marital or parental status but noticeable differences remain between the paid and unpaid work patterns of mothers and fathers.

In recent decades, globalization, technological change, freer trade agreements, and new government policies have altered labour markets and employment patterns for men and women. Women's employment rates still are influenced by their marital status, the financial need of their households, the age of their children, ideologies about women's role, opportunities to work part-time, and the availability of affordable child-care services, but they are also affected by national or local employment conditions. Some workers have benefited from globalizing labour markets, including young educated men and women who are childless and geographically mobile. Yet lone mothers and certain cultural minorities remain disproportionately represented among low-wage workers and low-income households.

In the past two decades, many firms, especially in the manufacturing sector, downsized to remain competitive in a world of freer trade and, in 2009, many more laid off workers and/or declared bankruptcy. Governments in the liberal welfare states no longer provide the same level of statutory protections for employees and unemployed workers, and labour forces have consequently become more polarized. Some families are 'work poor' or the adults are unemployed or marginally employed, while others are 'work rich' but have insufficient time for caring activities or leisure (Bittman, 1998; Torjman and Battle, 1999). The neo-liberal restructuring of paid work and the welfare state continues to aggravate the problems of the working poor, especially youth and lone mothers. Some governments have restricted eligibility to income support, arguing that nothing should prevent the rational unemployed person from finding and keeping work. Welfare-to-work programs imply that paid work is the answer to family poverty—but this can be true only when the job market is booming and wages are adequate relative to living costs.

Taylor-Gooby (2004) argued that new social risks have arisen from the decline of the male breadwinner family, labour market changes, and the impact of **globalization** on national policy-making. These new risks create challenges for governments as well as for youth, those without job skills, and women. They include balancing paid work and family responsibilities, being called on to care for a frail elderly relative, lacking the skills to find paid work with adequate wages, having skills that become obsolete, and using private provision that supplies insecure or inadequate services. Although balancing work and family is not exactly a new risk for women, the extent of the problem certainly has increased over the last generation as more married women have joined the workforce, as male wages have not kept up with living costs, and as the number of mother-led families continues to grow.

Although welfare states were established to deal with the risks of unemployment, sickness, disability, and retirement, the new risks provide complex challenges for governments (ibid.). They could expand public care for children and the elderly, promote more equal opportunities, and reduce employment poverty; but these solutions require agreement about the issues, considerable state intervention in the economy, and cooperation among governments, employers, unions, and voluntary organizations. New public spending would also require considerable political will to counteract the strong lobby from the political right that continues to argue for less government intervention and lower taxes.

Although governments are encouraging families to derive more of their income security from paid work, parents with the major responsibility for child care and housework enjoy fewer incentives to seek full-time employment or promotion. Many mothers cannot accept job assignments that involve moving to another city or country because they have to consider the lives of their partners and children. In addition, women's lower lifetime earnings increase their chances of poverty in old age, requiring state income support for many older unattached women. For this reason, governments are encouraging both women and men to see a lifetime of paid employment as normal; but not all women can easily do this unless family leave and caring arrangements are in place.

Summary

In this chapter, we see that as family members work longer hours for pay, family time becomes precious and more focused around employment needs while some household tasks and caring work are purchased on the market. The time that parents spend on caring activities reduces access to earnings and personal savings, but especially employed mothers are caught in a 'time crunch'. Who earns the household money also makes a difference to entitlement to spend it. Men normally have greater access to earnings than women but employed wives are more likely to maintain control over a portion of family money as well as their own earnings. The resources that governments invest in families to help bolster their earnings vary by country, but are relatively low in the liberal welfare states.

Questions for Critical Thought

1. Are wives and husbands entitled to the same family privileges when they become successful household earners?

2. Why is the gap between the earnings of mothers and childless women higher than the gender wage gap?

3. Do children and young people contribute their fair share to household work? Why or why not?

Suggested Readings

Atlantis: A Woman's Studies Journal. 2004. 'Never Done: The Challenge of Unpaid Work', Special issue 28, 2. This issue of a Canadian women's studies journal focuses on the value, gendering, and organization of unpaid work.

Pahl, Jan. 2005. 'Individualisation in Couple Finances: Who Pays for the Children?' *Social Policy and Society* 4, 4: 381–91. This article examines how couples manage their household money, showing that it has become more individualized.

Ranson, Gillian. 2009. 'Paid and Unpaid Work: How Do Families Divide Their Labour?', in M. Baker, ed., *Families: Changing Trends in Canada*, 6th edn. Toronto: McGraw-Hill Ryerson, 108–29. Ranson shows how shifts in the economy and how people earn their living affect the way that family life is organized. She also discusses the gendered division of caring work in Canada.

Suggested Websites

Childcare Resource and Research Unit *www.childcarecanada.org*
This University of Toronto site includes academic research and media coverage relating to child-care issues.

Organisation for Economic Development and Cooperation *www.oecd.org*
The website for this international organization contains many comparative statistics on paid work, child-care spending, and maternity benefits, especially through the project called *Babies and Bosses*.

Vanier Institute of the Family *www.vifamily.ca*
The Vanier Institute site offers information about employment trends of men and women, as well as material on family spending and debt.

Chapter 6

Separation, Divorce, and Re-partnering

Learning Objectives

- To relate the rising rates of separation and divorce to changes in the larger society
- To identify the impact of family law reforms on children and parents
- To discover whether re-partnering creates different kinds of families from first marriages

Chapter Outline

This chapter begins with a discussion of the rising rates of separation and divorce and the reasons for these trends. It also traces reforms in family and divorce laws—including those related to property, child custody, and child support—and examines the research on the outcomes of divorce and on experiences of living in stepfamilies.

Introduction

In the previous chapter, we saw that changing patterns of paid work have altered expectations about education and employment, the timing of marriage and child-bearing, and the division of labour between couples. More adolescents and parents now work longer hours, including evenings and on weekends, and aspirations for material wealth and career progression have increased. The growing percentage of the population working in insecure jobs and the increased choices about where to work also contribute to the impermanence of relationships. Even though most partners remain married for life, as we saw in Chapter 3, social researchers tend to focus on rising rates of marriage instability.

In this chapter, we explore why a higher percentage of couples now separate, why legal marriages span shorter periods of time than in previous decades, and how the experiences of children, mothers, and fathers differ in the 'post-divorce family'. These issues are not entirely academic ones as many of us have experienced either parental separation or the dissolution of our own marriages, while others have witnessed the separation of friends or siblings. These personal experiences may help to shape our understandings of the consequences of divorce, but we need to keep in mind that our own experiences may not be typical. However, personal knowledge might enhance our curiosity about the research findings relating to the separation and divorce outcomes of other people.

Why Are So Many Couples Separating?

When people get married, they usually intend to stay together for life. However, marriages are not lasting as long as they used to. A number of personal charac-teristics are correlated with higher rates of divorce, such as marrying someone from a different social background with varying ideas about the nature of mar-riage or preferable lifestyles. The probability of divorce also rises when couples marry early in life, household income is low, partners come from families with divorced parents, the woman gains high levels of education and income, part-ners are not religious, and when they cohabit before marriage (Bradbury and Norris, 2005; Wu and Schimmele, 2005, 2009). Bibby (2004–5) found that most Canadians look for certain characteristics in a partner and marry for a variety of reasons. However, the most prevalent reasons given for divorce were 'differ-ent values and interests' and 'abuse', as Table 6.1 indicates. This suggests that some partners either do not meet premarital expectations or they grow apart throughout the marriage.

In recent decades, the legal termination of marriage has more often been viewed as an acceptable conclusion to a relationship that has already broken down, and more people have come to appreciate that relationship dissolution does not necessarily arise from the misbehaviour of one partner. Instead, it stems from a variety of social and economic factors as well as personal ones, including less economic necessity to stay together if the marriage is unhappy and both partners can support themselves. Growing time pressures and perceptions of an unfair division of labour at home also contribute to resentment (especially from employed mothers) and in some cases lead to marriage dissolution.

Couples have their own personal reasons for separating but rates of separa-tion and divorce and the average duration of marriages that end in divorce vary regionally and cross-nationally, suggesting that societal factors alter these rates. For example, 38 per cent of all Canadian marriages can be expected to end in divorce before the thirtieth wedding anniversary, compared to 50 per cent of marriages in the province of Quebec (VIF, 2004: 33). The first year of marriage is often quite satisfying for couples but the likelihood of divorce rises abruptly in Canada until the fourth year of marriage. The mean duration of legal marriages

Table 6.1   Desired Characteristics in a Partner and Reasons for Marriage and Divorce

The Top Ten Characteristics That People Want in a Partner

1. Honesty
2. Kindness
3. Respect
4. Compatibility
5. Humour
6. Dependability
7. Love
8. Values
9. Religious commonality
10. Communication

The Top Eight Reasons Why People Want to Marry

1. Feeling that marriage signifies commitment
2. Moral values
3. Belief that children should have married parents
4. It is the natural thing to do
5. Financial security
6. Religious beliefs
7. Pressure from family
8. Pressure from friends

The Top Five Reasons Why People Want to Divorce

1. Different values and interests
2. Abuse—physical and emotional
3. Alcohol and drugs
4. Infidelity
5. Career-related conflict

Source: Bibby (2004). Reprinted by permission of the publisher.

ending in divorce is 14.2 years in Canada but only 8.3 years in Australia and as high as 19 years in Italy (OECD, 2005b: 33). As we will see later, cross-national differences in divorce rates and the duration of marriage are influenced by legal restrictions, cultural conditions, and religious considerations (ibid.).

From 1970 to 2001, average **divorce rates** tripled in OECD countries from 14.3 divorces per 100 marriages to 40.9 (OECD, 2001: 32; 2005b: 33). As Table 6.2 indicates, there is considerable variation in the divorce rates by country, from a low of 8.6 in Mexico to a high of 69.6 divorces per 100 marriages in Belgium in 2001

Table 6.2   Divorce Statistics in Selected OECD Countries, 2001

Country	Divorces per 100 Marriages	Mean Marriage Duration at Divorce
Australia	53.6	8.3
Belgium	69.6	13.0
Canada	48.5	14.2
Denmark	39.9	11.0
Finland	54.6	12.4
France	39.1	13.3
Germany	50.7	12.1
Ireland*	14.7	—
Italy	15.4	19.1
Mexico	8.6	—
Netherlands	46.6	12.2
New Zealand	48.5	13.0
Portugal	32.3	13.1
Spain*	18.2	16.1
Sweden	58.8	11.7
United Kingdom	54.8	10.9
United States	47.6	10.2
OECD average	40.9	11.9

*Spain passed divorce legislation in 1981 and Ireland in 1996.

Source: OECD (2005b: 33). Based on GE5.3. The ratio of divorces to marriages increased in most countries from 1995 to 2001. © OECD 2005.

(ibid.). In addition, divorce rates stabilized during the 1980s and 1990s in some countries (such as Canada) as cohabitation became more prevalent and legal marriage rates declined. Generally, separation rates (without legal divorce) are not available from government statistics because partners can walk away from their relationships without reporting the dissolution to the authorities. Nevertheless, demographers have estimated that if separations were added to current divorce rates, the figure could be four times as high as the official divorce rate, especially if we included separations from cohabitation (Beaujot, 2000: 110).

Higher rates of relationship breakdown have been influenced by a number of societal changes, including growing opportunities to live together outside marriage, changing attitudes about the 'right to happiness' in marriage, and liberalized divorce laws. Before the 1950s, both men and women needed marriage in order to survive economically, but since then the expansion of women's employment opportunities, public child-care services, and governments' income support programs have made it possible for both women and men to leave unhappy relationships and live outside marriage. Although women are more likely than men to initiate the separation (Amato and Previti, 2003; Hewitt et al., 2005), many separated mothers with young children struggle to make ends meet without a male earner in the household. Consequently, most governments have created state income support programs that enable lone mothers to recover from the emotional and financial trauma that often accompanies separation and to support their children while searching for paid work. Also, it is now easier for separated partners to live alone because of the availability of appliances, convenience food, self-contained apartments, and a variety of domestic services available on the commercial market.

Greater expectations of personal happiness and freedom of choice encourage people to leave unhappy relationships. People now feel less obligated to stay with their partners to fulfill their marriage vows, to please their parents, or to protect their reputations or those of their family. **Marital breakdown** has also become prevalent with increased geographic mobility and contact with people from different cultures. More **exogamy** or marriage outside one's social or cultural group means that an increasing percentage of partners enter marriage with different ideas about what constitutes a good couple relationship, positive relations with other family members, and a favourable lifestyle, which could augment marital conflict and eventually lead to separation.

Another reason for increased marriage breakdown is that laws in most countries now permit couples to divorce if one or both partners agree that their relationship has irretrievably broken down. Previously, divorce laws in common-law countries required legal proof presented in court to show that a partner had violated the marriage contract before the other partner could petition for divorce. This was a stressful, time-consuming, and expensive process. Now in many places, divorce is granted if the former partners state in writing that their marriage has broken down, as long as they wait a necessary period before applying for a divorce.

Reforms dealing with the division of matrimonial property, **child custody**, and **child support** have taken place in all the liberal welfare states. However, these legal changes have been controversial for a number of reasons: (1) they highlight deep-seated resentments about the different contributions husbands and wives typically make to household resources; (2) children in the 'post-divorce family' often live in impoverished households, despite recently acquired legal rights in all these countries and international conventions on the rights of the child from the United Nations; (3) parents often re-partner and scarce resources need to be shared among two or more households including biological and stepchildren; and (4) some critics suggest that liberalized divorce laws discourage couples from working harder to make their marriages work and argue that the grounds for divorce should be tightened once again.

In summary, more relationships and marriages now end because women and men have gained more opportunities to live outside marriage and because reformed divorce laws (combined with fewer children) make it easier for couples to separate. More people believe that they have the right to a satisfying marital relationship. If their current marriage is unhappy, they feel that they should not be forced to stay together and should be permitted to try again with a new partner. The rise in consensual relationships may have led to a stabilization or slight decline in divorce rates in some countries since the 1980s, but this does not mean that fewer relationships are dissolving. As we noted in Chapter 2, cohabiting couples have higher rates of separation than legally married couples. As more people cohabit, they contribute to family instability in the larger society (Beck-Gernsheim, 2002).

Separation Outcomes

Since the 1970s, the consequences of separation and divorce for men, women, and children have become controversial and the object of considerable public debate and policy research. Despite widespread agreement that spouses should not be forced to live together against their wishes, marriage and divorce trends have led to a number of concerns. These include the implications for children's behaviour and emotional well-being, the high poverty rates of mother-led families, the large percentage of 'fading fathers' who fail to visit their children and pay child support, and the allegations of court bias against fathers in custody and access awards.

After separation, most parents make their own decisions about child custody; if the courts in the common-law countries are asked to decide, they are expected to base their decisions on 'the best interests of the child'. However, who decides what is best for children and how do they arrive at this decision? In practice, most children continue to live with their mother after separation and divorce for a variety of reasons, discussed below. In Canada, for example, 80 per cent of lone-parent families were led by women in 2006, down from 83 per cent in 1981 (VIF, 2009). The minimum child support payment required by the liberal states is usually kept at a low level to encourage and enable low-income fathers to pay, but this means that it is often too small to pay the bills for the child's household. Furthermore, in the liberal welfare states many fathers fail to pay the required amount of child support and about one-third of fathers lose contact with their children altogether (Smyth, 2004). In most of these countries, the majority of divorced men re-partner and some produce additional children with new partners. Yet many fathers cannot earn enough to support two households with children.

Despite legal reform throughout the 1980s and 1990s, the courts have been unable to compensate for the gendered nature of paid and unpaid work during marriage, which clearly creates economic and social inequalities after separation. In addition, the courts are unable to compensate for the fact that two adult of divorces in 2002 (VIF, 2004: 37–8). However, when the courts do intervene, the trend towards joint custody in Canada is quite evident in official statistics. The percentage of children involved in awards of custody to both parents rose from 11.6 in 1986 to 41.8 in 2002, as Table 6.3 indicates. Yet, research suggests that joint custody is most effective when it is voluntary rather than enforced by the court (Baker, 1995: 300).

A number of countries (including Australia) have amended legislation to remove the word 'custody' or any other notions of child ownership from the language of divorce and to replace them with the words 'parental responsibilities' (Funder, 1996). Divorcing parents are also expected to make a parenting plan for their children with the assistance of counselling, conciliation, and mediation. Both parents now retain parenting responsibilities, yet mothers tend to remain the 'resident parent' and the main provider of daily care after separation and divorce.

The Australian 'Caring for Children after Separation' Project found that 79 per cent of children live with their mothers after separation (Qu, 2004). The relatively few children living with their fathers tend to be older, but no gender differences were apparent in this study. Smyth and Weston (2004) noted that less than six per cent of parents share the regular care of their children after separation, but that this arrangement is more likely to be preferred by fathers than by mothers, by parents already sharing care, and by non-resident parents rather than by resident parents. The attitudes of resident mothers towards **shared parenting** tend to be negative; mothers' attitudes become more positive in low-conflict parental relationships and for older children. Australian fathers reported that they *want* to be more involved in their children's lives after separation, perhaps a reaction to 'the apparent shallowness of every-other-weekend contact schedules that have arisen from traditional sole (maternal) custody models of post-separation parenting' (ibid., 14).

In the same study, researchers found that about 51 per cent of non-resident parents (mainly fathers) maintain regular face-to-face contact with their children after separation but 30 per cent retain little or no contact. Higher levels of contact between fathers and children were associated with lower levels of inter-

Table 6.3   Court-Ordered Custody Arrangements in Canada, 1986, 1995, and 2002

Custody arrangements	1986 %	1995 %	2002 %
Mother only	72.0	67.6	49.5
Joint custody (both mother and father)	11.6	21.4	41.8
Father only	15.3	10.9	8.5
Other	1.0	0.2	0.2

Source: Baker (1995: 300); VIF (2004: 38).

parental conflict, lower levels of **re-partnering**, less physical distance between the parents' households, and higher levels of financial resources (Smyth, 2004). Where father–child contact was tenuous, the perceptions of mothers and fathers differed. Mothers perceived that fathers lacked interest in the children while fathers felt that their former partners were cutting them out of the children's lives. This study shows that experiences and attitudes in the post-divorce family often vary by gender.

Box 6.1 The Attitudes of Separated Mothers and Fathers to 50/50 Shared Care

It is perhaps from the vantage point of being the primary caregivers of young children, and as a consequence being especially sensitive to children's needs, that mothers are more likely than fathers to oppose the idea of 50/50 care. They may perceive shared care to be too disruptive to children. On this issue, it is noteworthy that mothers' views about 50/50 care seemed to be influenced by their own children's ages and stages, and the level of inter-parental conflict.

For most fathers, the disconnection from their children that relationship breakdown often brings may be a central factor explaining the appeal of 50/50. Indeed, fathers' attitudes appeared to be tied in with their dissatisfaction with contact and with the decision-making processes that occurred in relation to contact. The strong desire by fathers for 50/50 care may reflect what Walker (2003: 403) calls a 'radiating message'. In this context, the message would be something like

> 'I want to be more involved in my children's lives', and may well be a reaction to the apparent shallowness of every-other-weekend contact schedules that have arisen from traditional (maternal) sole custody models of post-separation parenting. . .

Of course, the apparent simplicity of such gendered attitudinal data in relation to 50/50 care belies the complexity of parents' and children's needs and interests. Children's voices are needed on this issue, and are likely to add to this complexity.

Source: Smyth and Weston (2004: 14–15).

work and improving their circumstances. Curtis (2001) found that Canadian sole mothers typically reveal poorer health than married mothers, but when they controlled for age, income, education, lifestyle factors, family size, and other recognized determinants of health, the differences diminished.

Sarfati and Scott (2001) found that New Zealand sole mothers were more likely to have lower family incomes, lower educational qualifications, to be Maori, and to live in more deprived areas. They also found poorer physical and mental health among lone mothers, but the physical health differences disappeared after controlling for socio-economic variables. My own research based on qualitative interviews with 120 lone mothers on welfare in New Zealand illustrates their concerns when they are expected to find paid work despite having sick children, poor health of their own, multiple family problems, and depression. Their stories, which coincide with research in other countries, confirm that many of the liberal welfare states expect low-income mothers to find paid work and become self-supporting but offer them little social support to maintain their jobs and enhance their family well-being (Baker, 2002b; Baker and Tippin, 2004).

Whitehead et al. (2000) concluded that the Swedish social security system is more effective at keeping sole mothers healthier and out of poverty than the British system, yet Swedish sole mothers still report poorer mental and physical health than partnered mothers. These women may have experienced health problems before having a child, and the health issues could have contributed to marriage instability. In addition, the circumstances in which many lone mothers find themselves tend to contribute to depression and anxiety about the future. This anxiety could lead to problems disciplining children, especially if mothers have little support from family, friends, or social services. All these factors help to account for higher rates of behavioural problems in the children of lone mothers, especially those who are younger and never married.

Despite these findings, researchers have found no *direct* relationship between parental separation and children's adjustment, although many studies find differences between children from two-parent families and separated families (Amato and Keith, 1991; Burghes, 1994; Cartwright, 2008). Parental separation does add stress to children's lives through changes in relationships, living situations, and parental resources, but few studies conclude that psychological disturbance is severe or prolonged (Emery, 1994; Baker, 2007). It is difficult to determine, however, whether problems that surface later in adult life are attributable to parental divorce or other factors.

Woodward et al. (2000) analyzed longitudinal data from the Christchurch Health and Development Study in New Zealand. They found that exposure to parental separation was significantly associated with lower attachment to parents in adolescence and more negative perceptions of both maternal and paternal care and protection during childhood. The younger the child at the time of separation, the lower his or her subsequent parental attachment and the more likely the child was to perceive the parents as less caring but overprotective. Furthermore, other studies suggest that experiencing parental separation raises the chances of unstable relationships in adult life. This may result from poor relationship models in childhood, mistrust of the opposite sex learned from the custodial parent, or personal knowledge of divorce procedures and their aftermath.

Hughes (2005) used qualitative interviews with a small sample of Australian adults who had experienced parental separation as children to investigate some of the conclusions about the future of intimacy arising from the work of Giddens (1992) and Beck-Gernsheim (2002). These interviews suggested that experiencing parental separation may have a lasting impact by encouraging people to see intimate relationships as inherently fragile and to view the formation and termination of these relationships as part of their personal growth. Hughes's participants also saw the nuclear family as flawed and limited, especially in its potential to meet the needs of children. She concluded that if more people in the future live their lives outside the nuclear family in relatively 'loose formations', this will have 'monumental implications for public policy, and for the law in particular' (Hughes, 2005: 84).

Generally, we can assume that children are influenced by their home environment and their parents' relationships. Recent studies have found that the impact of parental marital experiences may become more apparent later in life in young people's attitudes about marriage, in their intimate relationships, and their relationships with parents and other family members (Cartwright, 2006, 2008; Cunningham and Thornton, 2006).

Remarriage and Stepfamilies

More people are entering legal marriage for the second or third time, particularly in countries with relatively high divorce rates. In Canada, Australia, and New Zealand, over one-third of all marriages involved at least one partner who had been previously married (Baker, 2001b: 21). Remarriage rates increased in these countries from the 1960s to the early 1990s, but as cohabitation increased and first marriage rates declined, remarriage rates have also declined. Nevertheless, more people are creating stepfamilies or **blended families** through re-partnering.

Stepfamilies have been described as the fastest-growing family form in the last few decades (Ferri and Smith, 2003; Doodson and Morley, 2006). Because most children live with the mother after separation, the most typical stepfamily arrangement involves a mother and her new partner living with her children, who are still maintaining contact with their non-resident father. In Canada, stepfamilies with children accounted for 12 per cent of all families with children in 2001. Of these families, 10 per cent contained only the children of the male spouse while 50 per cent contained only children of the female spouse. An additional 32 per cent of 'blended families' include children that the remarried couple produced together, while eight per cent contained no children (Statistics

Canada, 2002b). About half of stepfamilies in Canada are legally married while half are cohabiting. In Australia, four per cent of all families with children under the age of 18 are stepfamilies (with children brought to the relationship from either partner) and three per cent are blended families (with stepchildren and the biological children of the new couple) in 2006–07 (ABS, 2008c).

Despite the growth of stepfamilies, politicians, state officials, and social workers in many countries have expressed concern about the low remarriage rates among lone mothers. British research from the National Child Development Study found that 50 per cent of lone mothers re-partnered within three years if they had never been married, within about five years if divorced, and closer to eight years if they had been separated or widowed (McKay and Rowlingson, 1998). These figures are similar to but slightly longer than those reported from earlier studies from the United Kingdom (Ermisch, 1991) and longer than those found in American research. The duration of lone parenthood appears to be lengthening but is longer for mothers than fathers, for those living in social housing, and for men who are unemployed (McKay and Rowlingson, 1997).

Poor economic prospects, especially for young men, discourage marriage and remarriage among lone parents (ibid.). No financial advantage can be gained by a lone mother marrying an unemployed man, as her economic hardship could increase and she might disqualify herself from state income support. In addition, re-partnering does not necessarily lead to better child development, although it usually constitutes an economic gain for the lone mother and her children if the man is employed.

Children in stepfamilies have been found to have higher rates of accidents, higher levels of bedwetting, more contact with the police, and lower self-esteem, and to leave school earlier without qualifications compared to children in lone-parent families (Wadsworth et al., 1983; Elliott et al., 1993; Beaupré et al., 2006). Pryor and Rodgers (2001) argue that these experiences can be explained by the lower family aspirations and expectations that step-parents have for their step-children compared to their own biological children, as well as by family friction in these households. Stepfamilies also involve more conflict than lone-parent families because they include more than two sets of adults (both resident and absent parents) as well as children from different parents and social backgrounds, who are all supposed to live together amicably. In addition, stepfamilies often experience more financial problems, especially when fathers are supporting children in more than one household. These financial difficulties may lead to more general disputes about the fair allocation of resources, time, and attention. Researchers also note that young children fare better than older children in stepfamilies because adaptation is easier at an earlier age before allegiances are developed to the absent parent. Research on stepfamilies report that the role of stepmother is more ambiguous and stressful than the role of stepfather, and find that mothers are described as being more negative towards step-parenting than are fathers (Cheal, 1996; Doodson and Morley, 2006; Schodt, 2008).

Stepfamily formation has been viewed as another stressful event to cope with for children who were not involved with their parents' decision to separate any more than they were party to their parent's decision to re-partner (Smith, 2004). While the new household members need to learn to be a functioning family unit, the relationship between the children and their non-resident father usually continues, even though it may change. Researchers agree that prolonged conflict between parents has a negative impact on the children, but they disagree about how feelings of closeness with biological fathers influence children's acceptance of stepfathers. Some studies suggest that children who develop strong bonds with their biological fathers may feel that forming a relationship with their stepfather would be disloyal to their biological father. However, most researchers have found little correlation (ibid.).

The Study of Stepchildren and Step-Parenting in the United Kingdom was a large cross-sectional study of stepfamilies living in and around London from one to four years between 1998 and 2002. Smith (2004) reported on children's views about contact with their non-resident fathers and the quality of relationships with their fathers and stepfathers using data from this study. 67 per cent of children reported contact with their non-resident parents within the past year. More frequent contact (at least monthly) was associated with children's perceptions of a 'good quality relationship' and with their father behaving in a 'normal way' rather than focusing mainly on treats and special activities.

Contrary to some American findings from the 1980s, the British study found no evidence that having a good relationship with the biological father precludes having a good relationship with the stepfather (Smyth, 2004). In fact, the authors concluded that children who have strong relationships with their mothers and non-resident fathers are more likely to develop good relationships with their stepfathers. More generally, Smith concluded that children who are well-adjusted and have a positive self-image are more likely to form positive relationships with those around them. New Zealand research reported by Pryor (2004) also confirmed this finding. As stepfamilies are a growing family type in all the liberal states, research is expanding rapidly on this topic (Pryor, 2008; Shriner, 2009).

Conclusion

Since the 1960s, the common-law countries have experienced similar socio-demographic trends relating to relationship breakdown, including higher separation rates, more mother-led families, high rates of poverty in mother-led families, higher re-partnering rates, and well-publicized parental disputes over child support, custody, and access. In response to the political pressure arising from these trends, the common-law countries liberalized their divorce laws and developed **gender-neutral** laws relating to divorce, support, and child custody. In deciding where the post-divorce child should live, these countries continue to emphasize the 'best interests of the child'. Cooperation between parents over access and care arrangements is encouraged, and the family courts include mediation and less adversarial practices than courts for dealing with non-family matters.

Despite these reforms, controversies continue. Mothers usually retain the daily care of their children after marriage breakdown but nearly half of mother-led households live on low incomes in Canada and some English-speaking countries (OECD, 2008a). Since the 1980s, non-resident fathers have gained more legal rights to make decisions about their children's welfare and more divorced fathers now maintain contact with their children. However, about a third of non-resident fathers lose contact. Child-support enforcement laws have been tightened, making more fathers pay, but the state has been unable to retrieve the full amount of financial support from all fathers required to pay.

In the past few decades, numerous researchers from a variety of disciplines have investigated various aspects of marriage breakdown and its social and economic outcomes. They have concluded that high rates of separation and divorce reflect the rise of individualism, the greater **secularization** of society, and the growing view that relationships should last only as long as they are mutually satisfying. However, high rates of re-partnering suggest that intimate cohabitation is still desired and valued. Furthermore, it is still the case that most people aspire to committed and permanent relationships and that most couples remain married for life.

If we add together legal marriages, remarriages, consensual heterosexual relationships, and same-sex cohabitation, we could argue that the percentage of people living in intimate partnerships remains as high as ever. However, fewer partners are willing to remain in unhappy relationships for an extended time. The desire for intimacy remains strong, but more social and economic forces work against the durability of relationships, including labour market trends, greater geographic mobility, gendered patterns of paid and unpaid work, and new ideas about creating personal biographies. Both the legitimation and the rising prevalence of separation and divorce continue to present challenges to former partners, families, communities, social service agencies, and the welfare state.

Summary

In recent decades, more marriages and relationships are ending in separation. Laws have been reformed to acknowledge that marriages do not necessarily last for life and to help separating couples decide on care arrangements and the division of family assets. However, the law assumes more gender equity than exists in reality, especially in regard to the ability of mothers with young children to become self-supporting after divorce. This chapter argues that the increased impermanence of marriage has transformed family life for many.

Questions for Critical Thought ——————————

1. Does parental separation or divorce influence young people's experiences with intimate relationships later in life?

2. Why do so many separated and divorced fathers absent themselves from their children's lives?

3. Is divorce more likely to occur if young people enter marriage with the knowledge that divorce is relatively easy, both socially and legally?

Suggested Readings ——————————

Ambert, Anne-Marie. 2005. *Divorce: Facts, Causes and Consequences*. Ottawa: Vanier Institute of the Family, www.vifamily.ca. This online resource summarizes a large amount of research on families in Canada and the United States.

Pryor, Jan, and Bryan Rodgers. 2001. *Children in Changing Families: Life after Parental Separation*. Oxford: Blackwell. This book covers international research on the impact of parental separation and stepfamily formation on children, and offers insights into why some survive family change better than others.

Wu, Zheng, and Christophe Schimmele. 2009. 'Divorce and Repartnering', in M. Baker, ed. *Families: Changing Trends in Canada*, 6th edn. Toronto: McGraw-Hill Ryerson, 154–78. This chapter provides a historical perspective on divorce in Canada and discusses divorce outcomes for various family members.

Suggested Websites ——————————

Australian Institute of Family Studies *www.aifs.gov.au*
    This organization has been carrying out research for several decades on a number of family issues, including separation and divorce and its impact on children.

Journal of Divorce and Remarriage *www.haworthpress.com*
    This interdisciplinary academic journal is an authoritative resource on all aspects of separation, divorce, single parenting, remarriage, and stepfamilies.

Chapter 7

Midlife, Aging, and Retirement

Learning Objectives

- To reinforce the idea that aging is partially 'socially constructed' as its meaning varies over time, social class, gender, and culture
- To acknowledge that midlife often brings new challenges as paid work intensifies, more marriages end, children stay at home longer, and parents sometimes require care
- To provide an overview of research findings about lasting marriages and grandparenting
- To understand how income varies by age and employment status, and how governments have supported the well-being of elderly persons

Chapter Outline

This chapter discusses the socially constructed meaning of aging and how the life cycle and midlife has changed over the decades. It also examines the research on marriage longevity, grandparenting, and retirement income.

Introduction

In this chapter, we discuss the various portrayals of aging in the media, in advertising, public discourse, social programs, and academic research. The meaning of aging changes with our own chronological age, but also with rising life expectancies and visible indicators of fitness, health, and activity level among middle-aged and older people. This chapter suggests that the lives of the middle aged and elderly are often presented in somewhat misleading and biased ways. For example, recent advertising usually presents older people mainly as heterosexual couples, who live in retirement villages, dote on their grandchildren, take luxurious cruises around the world, and continue to enjoy a strong sex life. In contrast, much of the social and health research focuses on poor health, care problems of the frail elderly, elder abuse, and loneliness and poverty in old age. Few academic studies discuss unmarried elderly people or gay and lesbian elderly. Political discourse tends to concentrate on retirement policies, eligibility for pensions, and, more recently, on grandparent responsibilities for neglected or abused grandchildren.

In reality, increasing age often brings higher incomes and assets, career progression, growing satisfaction with family and friends, and considerable emotional and material assistance to children and grandchildren. Most middle-aged and elderly people report good health, have wide social networks, and live in their own homes in ordinary communities. More men and women now work in the labour force until older ages than previous decades, and most remain active and enjoy good health well beyond their 60s and 70s. Although older couples are now more likely to divorce than in the past, most marriages still last a lifetime. Most people over the age of 60 are parents and grandparents, but a growing minority live alone, have re-partnered, or live as same-sex couples. Some of these social myths are addressed in this chapter but we first examine the changing social meanings attributed to aging.

The Changing Meaning of Aging

Ideas about appropriate behaviour, appearance, and relationships for older people have changed considerably over the centuries and especially in the last few decades. As life expectancy has increased, so has the meaning of 'old age' and 'elderly', although the definitions of these concepts seem to vary with our own age. For example, when we were children, a 25-year-old seemed old, but when turning 50, your definition of old age might rise to 70 or 80 years. When you are 90, a person aged 75 might be considered a 'youngster'. So perceptions of aging are related to our personal circumstances but social scientists can also see patterns in aging and the social circumstances of the elderly based on gender, social class, culture, and changes in the larger society. Furthermore, some organizations and agencies continue to make profits from focusing on the needs of youth, the middle aged, or the elderly, and adjust their advertising, publicity, or lobbying towards the interests of these groups.

The fashion and cosmetics industries have convinced many women (and a growing number of men) to spend large amounts of time, effort, and money attempting to look younger than their chronological age. Although physical fitness and fashionable clothing have always been important to some people, a youthful appearance seems to be valued more for women than men in today's society (Abu-Laban and McDaniel, 1998; Winterich, 2007). Some women attempt to maintain the appearance and feeling of youthfulness with the assistance of hair colouring, skin treatments, cosmetic surgery, expensive clothing, hormone replacement therapy, diets, and exercise. Advertisers often use images of youthful and sexy women to sell a variety of products, especially those targeted to men.

Women are encouraged to believe that a youthful and glamorous appearance is essential for their self-esteem, their friendships, and their ability to find and retain (heterosexual) intimate relationships. The 'marriage gradient' actually shows that older men often cohabit with and marry much younger women but the reverse seldom occurs, which indicates that men's older age may actually become an asset (especially if he is also rich and famous) while women's advanced age may become a liability on the dating or marriage market. However, social class, education, and culture tend to be intervening variables in the quest for eternal youth.

In some occupations requiring wisdom or expertise, women and men might attempt to look older than their chronological age or at least settle for looking their age. In contrast, older people working in the fashion industry or the media might want to look younger than they really are. Affluent people seem better able to use their financial resources and education to remain healthier, more active, and to live longer than those on lower incomes, who often look older through years of hard work, poor nutrition, or stressful lives. Those with higher incomes are able to live in spacious and well-heated houses in safer communities, and are able to buy more nutritious food, preventive health care services, and supervision for their children and other family members in need of care. Richer people are also less likely to work outdoors or to smoke and to drink alcohol to excess, which contributes to a younger appearance (Wister, 2005). Certain cultural groups also place a higher value on 'active aging', take regular exercise, keep their weight down, enjoy adequate leisure time, and travel widely in later life, although this may partially relate to their social class as well as culture.

Generally, sociologists would argue that the meanings associated with chronological age are socially constructed, and the outcomes of chronological aging reflect the socio-economic and cultural circumstances of people's earlier lives. Many older people also seem to look younger and more fit than they did a few generations ago. This has led people to revise earlier ideas about typical patterns of aging.

Life Expectancy, the Life Cycle, and Aging

Since the 1930s, life expectancy has increased in most developed countries as a result of improvements in sanitation, accommodation, diet, and health care. Health improvements include the development of inoculations against contagious diseases, the invention of antibiotics, and advances in maternal health. Life expectancy at birth varies by country but in industrialized nations such as Canada and the United States, women tend to live longer than men. In past decades, the gender gap in life expectancy has widened from 5.0 years in 1960 to 5.7 years in 2004 (OECD, 2007: 88). Life expectancies also vary by social class (Whitehouse and Zaidi, 2008).

The growing gender gap in life expectancy can be attributed to the decline of maternal death rates or safer childbirth, as well as higher premature death rates among males, which are influenced by lifestyle factors, access to health care services, and cultural practices. In most countries, girls and boys are socialized to develop different interests and activities, and boys are often encouraged to take more risks, first in play and later in work and leisure. Gendered patterns are also apparent in activities reducing life expectancy, such as cigarette smoking, the use of illegal drugs, excessive alcohol consumption, reckless driving of motor vehicles, and working in dangerous jobs. The gender differences in life expectancy are augmented within families because men tend to marry or cohabit with younger women, and wives normally outlive their husbands.

Stages in the life cycle are now becoming less distinct than in previous decades. Prior to the Second World War, many people left school, worked for several years, married, raised children, saw their children grow and leave home, retired from paid work (or saw their partner retire), and helped raise their grandchildren. Now, more people reproduce outside of marriage, they partner and re-partner, begin new families in mid-life or old age, move in and out of jobs, retire and return to paid work, or retain their paid jobs as long as possible.

Generational differences are apparent in typical patterns of aging. People born after the Second World War (the post-war baby boomers) tend to be better educated than previous generations. On average, their post-secondary degrees and diplomas enabled them to find higher-paying jobs and, with the assistance of credit cards and the two-earner family, they came to expect higher living standards. They are more likely than their parents to travel internationally, to engage in regular exercise, to have experienced more than one marriage, to take adult education courses, to question authority, and to become more articulate about their needs as they grow older.

The post-war generation (born 1945–65) grew up with a variety of social security programs. Unlike their parents, this generation felt less need to save their money in case of unemployment, ill health, or disability in old age. They continued to consume at a higher rate than their parents' generation, with the expectation that social security benefits would continue and that credit would always be available. The post-war generation may live longer and healthier lives than their parents' generation, as they were fortunate to grow up with better nutrition, sanitation, and health services, and with an increased knowledge of the relationship between fitness, nutrition, smoking, and health. On the other hand, environmental pollution, obesity, high rates of smoking and substance abuse, and new strains of viruses could curtail this optimistic scenario.

Throughout the 1980s and 1990s, many men retired before age 65, earlier than previous generations, and lived off private savings and investments, employer-sponsored pension benefits, and public pensions. Now, however, more men and women are once again remaining in the labour force longer, with increasing uncertainty about incomes and pensions, declining house prices, lower interest rates, fewer private savings, and higher levels of household debt. Many people will continue working until their mid-60s or 70s, either to acquire adequate retirement incomes or because they enjoy their work and the social interaction with their workmates.

Post-war baby-boomers will probably place less emphasis than previous generations on individualism in their old age because many have relied throughout their lives on government assistance or formal services as well as their own initiative. With fewer children than their parents' generation, they may need to purchase more assistance in old age. With higher levels of education and more experience with hiring help, they may become more demanding about the quality of services than the elderly in the past. With the post-2008 recession, however, many older workers could be made redundant before they have paid off their mortgages or saved enough money for a comfortable retirement.

The cohort of people born after the 1970s will likely experience a different scenario of aging. They may be less able to afford retirement from paid work because they have worked part-time for larger portions of their lives, changed jobs more frequently, separated from partners and divided family assets, and accrued substantial personal and household debt. Many will be unable to depend on home ownership as a form of retirement savings, and they may be less likely to have work-related pensions or personal savings to permit retirement. In addition, they may have less confidence in the future of public pensions or government services for the elderly.

In the twenty-first century, most adults still reproduce and later become grandparents when their adult children reproduce (Mann, 2007). Relationships between grandparents and their grandchildren could become more salient as life expectancies rise and these relationships have longer to develop. On the other hand, the trend toward delayed childbirth will mean that some children will be relatively young when their grandparents die, as the years between generations lengthen. Furthermore, young people are now more mobile and often move far away from their parents. In addition, the divorce and re-partnering of adult children prevents many grandparents from developing close relationships with their grandchildren.

Some social scientists have suggested that rapid social change and population aging encourage intergenerational conflict between the young who are competing for jobs and resources and the older workers who want to hold onto their jobs. However, the young and the middle-aged ultimately have a vested interest in improving pensions and services for the elderly. The real conflict is more likely between organizations and especially commercial companies that cater to the needs of, or benefit from, a youthful population and those whose interests lie with the elderly. Many of our social organizations such as schools and universities, which have based their funding policies on growing numbers of students (or 'bums on seats'), will fight to change the funding formulae when these are no longer to their advantage. Improved conditions for the elderly will eventually benefit individuals, families, and communities, but not necessarily all public or private organizations.

Even a generation ago, social scientists talked about 'the family life cycle' as though everyone went through the same stages of family development at the same time. Now, rising rates of cohabitation, separation, divorce, re-part-nering, lifelong learning, and the need to find new ways to earn a living have disrupted the typical life stages of the past.

Mid-Life: Is it a Time of Security or Crisis?

In popular culture, mid-life has been associated with aging 'crises' for both men and women but in reality, these are myths for most people (Pool and Feldman, 1999). Increasingly, both men and women are employed during their middle years and their earnings may peak during their late 40s and 50s. Rates of home and car ownerships are the highest, assets are at their peak, but debts are generally declining, as Table 7.1 indicates for Canada. Generally, mid-life has been a time of greater financial security for most people in Canada and the other liberal welfare states, although this is rapidly changing.

In the past when many men worked for one employer for life, they might be tiring of their job by the time they reached their 50s. Now, fewer men stay in the same occupation for life, with less employment permanence and more desire to seek better opportunities elsewhere. Middle-aged women are also likely to be in the full-time workforce, especially in North America, and most of these women are stable workers who are gaining in seniority and earnings and making an important contribution to household income. Two-earner families are likely to have the most financial security (Sauvé, 2009).

For women, midlife also corresponds with menopause, which involves not only physiological changes but which may also contribute to thoughts and concerns about growing old. When more middle-aged women devoted their lives to child-bearing and child-rearing, menopause and children leaving home could more readily be perceived as synonymous with the end of their useful-ness. Now, midlife for mothers often means a reduction of responsibilities for child supervision and if the children are no longer living at home, it could mean less daily housework such as food shopping, meal preparation, and laundry. A reduction of domestic work permits women to spend more time and effort on other activities, such as their paid jobs.

Clearly, both men and women look and feel different as they grow older. Men are less likely than women to colour their greying hair or to have cosmetic surgery, but many men are nevertheless concerned about their weight and physical fitness, about their sexual prowess, about the quality of their intimate

Table 7.2   Age-Specific Divorce Rates in Australia, 1988 and 2007 (divorces per 1,000 population of the same age in mid-year)

Age Group	1988		2007	
	Male	Female	Male	Female
24 and under	1.2	2.8	0.3	0.8
25–29	9.4	12.7	3.9	6.4
30–34	12.8	12.9	8.4	9.9
35–39	12.3	11.6	10.2	11.0
40–44	11.0	10.0	10.4	10.8
45–49	9.2	7.8	10.2	9.4
50–54	6.7	4.6	8.6	7.2
55–59	4.3	2.7	6.8	4.7
60–64	2.6	1.6	4.6	2.8
65 and over	1.1	0.4	1.6	0.6

Source: Australian Bureau of Statistics (2008). Available at http://www.abs.gov.au/ausstats/abs@.nsf/mf/3307.0.55.001?OpenDocument

over 45 years of age (ABS, 2008). Because older men often marry younger women, women's marriage and divorce rates at older ages are lower than men's. However, more women than men still petition for divorce, although joint petitions are on the rise in Australia (ABS, 2008). In addition, more separated and divorced people re-partner and establish new households without legally marrying. However, remarriage remains more popular than cohabitation among older couples, especially those who are more affluent and have children. Older re-partnering parents often experience concerns about joint property, pension entitlement, inheritance, and providing role models of committed relationships for their children.

Part of the reason for rising separation and divorce rates among older couples relates to economic opportunities. Having individual earnings provides new options for women in mid-life, and those in unhappy marriages are able to separate and divorce because both they and their former partner have more financial resources to live independently. Nevertheless, we saw in Chapter 6 that former wives are less likely than former husbands to prosper economically after divorce, and less likely to re-partner. Neither children's living arrangements nor women's incomes relative to men have changed much in recent years, and custodial or resident mothers continue to live on lower incomes than their male counterparts. The shortage of suitable male partners and women's time spent caring for children reduce the probability of female remarriage in later life. In addition, women appear less eager than men to remarry because more women experienced non-reciprocal experiences as partners and carers throughout marriage (Poole, 2005; Ranson, 2009). Although more middle-aged and older people now leave unhappy marriages, most couples stay together regardless of the quality of their marriage—out of loyalty, concern about their children, fear of loneliness or loss of social networks, or from financial pressures.

One of the reasons why people marry and reproduce is to widen their social networks, create companionship and emotional support for life, and reduce the fear of loneliness in later life. However, about one-quarter of people in the liberal welfare states do not become parents or grandparents. Researchers have asked if older parents are more socially integrated or do older childless couples simply replace their lack of children with more friends? Dykstra (2006) found in her research in Germany and the Netherlands that people who never had children had smaller social networks in old age but more contact with peers of the same generation, including siblings, friends, colleagues, cousins, and neighbours. However, over time, these networks diminish as age peers die or move away. In contrast, parents become grandparents and develop expanding networks of relatives.

Grandparenting

About three-quarters of the population of countries such as the United Kingdom become grandparents during their lifetime, and they remain grandparents for an average of 25 years (Mann, 2007). Many people become grandparents when they are in their 40s or 50s, when they are still at work, or involved with other activities. Grandparenting is often described as an 'affective role' but it has become more heterogeneous over the decades, especially with high rates of separation, divorce, and re-partnering. Most grandparents see their grandchildren regularly but a small minority (about 10 per cent in the United States) take over the daily care of their grandchildren because their children are unable to care for them because of alcohol or drug abuse or work-related pressures (Mann, 2007). Other grandparents remain detached and distant. Increasingly, adult children move away from their parents for education and work, and some grandparents rarely see their grandchildren because of the geographic distance. However, they may still remain in regular communication with them. Levels of involvement with grandchildren seem to be greater when grandchildren are very young compared to when they are teenagers but it may also vary by the grandparents' age, health, other activities, class background, and geographic proximity (Gauthier, 2002; Harper, 2005).

Much of the research on grandparenting focuses on grandmothers, either implicitly or explicitly (Harper, 2005), partly because grandmothers have served as the principal grandparent and spent more time in physical and emotional care of their grandchildren. Grandmothers often expect to spend time both with their children and grandchildren, especially during holidays and celebrations, and frequently 'babysit' their grandchildren for at least some of the time while suitable, available, or affordable. Furthermore, many families, especially those in certain cultural communities, feel that using these services would be the same as abandoning their parents to an uncaring and inflexible living arrangement.

Rising life expectancies, smaller families, and re-partnering have broadened the responsibilities of some people in mid-life. While young people are remaining in their parents' home for longer, some people have responsibilities for their partner's children and parents, and many seniors are living well into their 80s and 90s. This means that more middle-aged parents may retain some responsibility for two generations—their children and their parents. But they may also retain some responsibility for their partner's parents as well (or even their ex-partner's parents). Adults may begin to help out their older relatives gradually, such as cutting the lawn or helping with income tax returns or financial decision-making, and gradually take over more tasks such as driving them grocery shopping or to have a haircut, and finally doing housework and assisting with personal care.

Although governments and private agencies have developed home and community care services, such as visiting homemakers and meals-on-wheels, these tend to be under-funded by governments in the liberal welfare states such as Australia, Canada, New Zealand, United Kingdom, and the United States. The majority of public funding still is allocated to acute-care hospitals and medical services rather than community or home care. Although more senior residences are being built, some with meals, entertainment, and personal care services, many are privately-run, expensive, and have long waiting lists. Also, many seniors prefer to remain in their own homes without moving to age-homogeneous accommodation, especially if they feel that they are relatively healthy and able to cope with personal care. Yet their children or younger relatives may not agree that they can adequately care for themselves and may feel obligated to help out.

Easing the family's responsibilities for the care of frail elderly parents or other relatives may require the reallocation of government funding into long-term care and community services rather than hospital-based medical services. In addition, respite care programs allow family carers to leave their parent with an alternative care provider for the day while they attend to other matters. Programs to assist family care giving should focus on perceptions of need as well as actual requirements, and encourage and enable elderly people to retain their independence for longer. Some governments already provide a range of services for seniors, such as home renovations for persons with disabilities, home repair services, cleaning services, and home security checks. The cost to the user is sometimes based on one's ability to pay, which means they are subsidized by the taxpayer. However, the liberal welfare states seem less willing to pay for these services than the social democratic states such as Sweden and Denmark (Cates, 1993; Caro, 2006; OECD, 2007).

Does Aging Make People More Conservative?

For decades, sociologists have questioned whether people become more conservative as they grow older or if each **cohort** experiences aging differently because of earlier circumstances and life events. Most sociological studies of aging compare different generations living at the same time rather than several generations throughout their entire life span, so we cannot say that social differences between age groups are the result of the aging process. Intergenerational variations could be caused by the political, economic, and social conditions during childhood, adolescence, or early adulthood. Certainly the generation that is now over 65 years of age has grown up in a different social and economic world than today's youth, who will be the elderly of the future.

The lives of many of today's seniors, or those who have recently died, were greatly influenced by the 1930s' Depression and the Second World War. The Depression may have curtailed their education, delayed their marriage, or forced them to accept financially secure but unchallenging work. Trying to make ends meet during those years encouraged thrift, financial anxiety, and caution. Travelling overseas during wartime may have been their first opportunity to see the world, to leave their hometown, and make some money, as well as to serve their country. Yet many surviving veterans and refugees, as well as their families, were changed forever by the destruction of war, the death of their relatives and friends, food rationing, loneliness, and subsequent injuries or disabilities. Both the Depression and the Second World War made lasting impressions on today's elderly, altering their attitudes, expectations, behaviour, and relationships.

Past generations needed to be prepared for life's unexpected events in a way that young people born after the 1960s find difficult to comprehend. Today's seniors had to prepare themselves for the future by saving money, maintaining a support network of friends and family, or by cultivating an attitude of resignation because they lacked social security programs, health insurance, bank credit, reliable birth control, or personal choices. Many of today's elderly relied on hard work and family loyalty, and hoped that their children would feel a reciprocal responsibility to assist them later in life. Nevertheless, most elderly couples live independent lives and many provide volunteer work for their communities as well as child care and financial assistance for their adult children.

Those born in the liberal welfare states after the Second World War were raised to take income security programs, private insurance, government medical insurance, inflation, and financial credit for granted. They felt less compelled to save for the future, to 'defer gratification', or to stay in unsatisfying jobs or unhappy marriages out of duty or obligation. They were more likely to flaunt social rules, to move in and out of jobs and relationships, to live for the present freeze sperm means that conception can happen after the donor or father's death. In addition, 'designer babies' are possible, post-menopausal women can have babies, and wealthy couples can commission low-income women to produce children for them (Eichler, 1997). Although these new reproductive practices are not yet very prevalent, they are widely discussed in the media, and the very possibilities alter our ways of thinking about sex, reproduction, and childbirth.

Innovations in transportation technology also influence family life. The invention of automobiles early in the twentieth century permitted more privacy and intimacy for 'courting' couples. The widespread use of automobiles also altered patterns of residence, allowing people to live farther from work and to purchase a holiday home, and encouraged more travel for both work and leisure. Now, many families own more than one car, which increases household costs but enables couples to work in different locations farther from home. International travel is also more feasible because of lower airfares relative to wages. Affordable and faster international travel permits more people to take overseas holidays, to maintain contact with friends and family abroad, and to study or work in other countries. It also enables them to flee from family conflict or abusive partners and to find a safe haven in other jurisdictions. However, new computerized surveillance technologies and multilateral agreements between governments assist officials to apprehend parents who cross borders to shirk their family responsibilities (Baker, 2006).

More family members are now spread throughout the world and immigrants arrive from a larger range of countries with different family practices (OECD, 2005b). Although this increases diversity, research suggests that especially young migrants and the second generation modify their family demography to make it more consistent with patterns in their adopted country (Albanese, 2009). Nevertheless, more young people in Western countries have parents and grandparents living in arranged marriages, dressing in traditional clothes, and eating a wider variety of foods. Many migrants maintain regular contact with relatives back home through e-mail, long-distance telephone calls, electronic financial transfers, and regular air travel. Some parents even earn money in one place and raise children in another, and small percentages become 'transnational citizens' who are equally comfortable living in several countries.

Cell phones and e-mail help family members and friends to maintain contact and permit parents to 'supervise' their children from a distance, even while working. Television and the Internet bring international news and advertising into our homes, spreading a more cosmopolitan outlook but also introducing us to new forms of consumerism that tend to raise our material aspirations. The Internet also enables global marketing, the rapid spread of news, international lobbying, chat groups, sexual encounters, and new dating practices, but also the dissemination of pornography and stalking. Technology increasingly permeates our sexual practices, child-rearing, the maintenance of relationships, the design of our homes, and patterns of work and leisure, introducing new ideas and irritations into our lives.

Increasingly, people around the world watch the same television programs and films, read the same books and material on the Internet, and view the same images and advertisements, although the 'globalization of culture' consists largely of Western ideas from the United States, the United Kingdom, and Europe circulating to the rest of the world (Baker, 2006). Young people in remote or less developed areas can be enticed by these images and ideas, and may try to simulate the fashions and lifestyles of the West. Consequently, more people expect to choose where they live and with whom, what they buy, how they will earn a living, and how they spend their leisure time. Westernization tends to encourage contraceptive use, freer choice of marriage partners, nuclear family living, a greater acceptance of divorce, and the desire for more gender equality within marriage (Giddens, 1992).

New ideas about human rights, gender equity, family obligations, and entitlement to social benefits also shape expectations and family patterns in subtle ways (Baker, 2006). Policy reforms may initially force people to conform, but also to change their expectations over time and eventually alter their behaviour. Restructuring social programs may also help shape gender relations, the meaning of 'good parenting', and expectations about future social provision. Recently, governments in the liberal welfare states have encouraged both mothers and fathers to view paid employment as the normal activity for all adults, even though they have not always provided the necessary facilities or subsidies for child care.

Throughout this book I have argued that even though we can now exercise more choice in our personal lives, few of the new family patterns are entirely matters of individual choice. Our behaviour and even our personal ambitions tend instead to be influenced and modified by social and economic activities and events in the larger society, and these are difficult for individuals to control. Constraints on relationships may relate to lack of money or power, new legal requirements, technological 'advances', pressures from family and friends, and feelings of obligation or entitlement. Personal constraints can arise simply from the wishes or actions of a partner. For example, we might choose to live in an egalitarian relationship but if our partner refuses to share the household earnings or the domestic work, we cannot have what we want. We may choose to grow old with our partner, but if he or she leaves us, our own personal preferences may no longer be relevant.

It is difficult to anticipate how we would react to particular changes in our personal lives, such as an unexpected pregnancy or a separation, or how or where we will be living in 20 years. It is even more challenging for social scientists to predict future family patterns.

Predicting Future Family Patterns

Two important goals of science are to identify patterns and accurately predict future trends. Within the social sciences, predicting human behaviour seems complicated because so many factors are involved, such as new ideas, technological changes, economic and political transformations, labour market transitions, legal and policy changes, emotions, and personal choices. Researchers attempting to predict family trends have often relied on past and current demographic patterns as social indicators of the future, but human beings also can choose to resist prevailing family patterns and to contravene socially acceptable behaviour. Consequently, predictions have not always been accurate, especially when researchers rely mainly on demographic trends. A successful prediction of personal and family life requires some knowledge of social psychology, political movements, policy reform, economic trends, technological innovations, and popular culture.

Despite the challenges of prediction in the social sciences, the rest of this chapter suggests the family patterns that are likely to continue into the future. These ideas, portrayed in Table 8.1, have been garnered from research on family demography, new forms of relationships, changing labour market trends, and the restructuring of public policy. However, the trends pertain only to people living in Western industrialized countries and especially the **liberal welfare states** of Australia, Canada, New Zealand, the United States, and the United Kingdom. In addition, these predictions stretch only a few decades into the future because it is so difficult to know how socio-economic and political life might change. Nevertheless, this exercise should enable us to draw some conclusions about the nature of family life and the power of certain constraints on our personal choices.

Will People Still Get Married?

Compared to the 1950s, more people are now sexually active outside marriage, more couples cohabit without legal ceremony, and the average age of marriage has been rising. At the same time, we have seen that live-in relationships without legal ceremonies have a shorter duration and more end in separation. In the next two decades, these trends will likely continue and even accelerate. More people will come to believe that their personal and intimate life is their own affair, with little relevance to religious leaders or civil authorities. Advanced birth control technology will continue to enable couples to enjoy sexual activity without pregnancy or marriage, and the social and legal differences between cohabitation and legal marriage will diminish even further. In addition, ideas about the right to privacy and personal happiness will continue to pervade much of Western culture, shaping patterns in sexuality and family formation. With the decline in the economy and rising unemployment, however, some individuals will become

Table 8.1   Future Trends in Family Life

Area of Family Life	Future Trend
Cohabitation	• Rates will rise among all age groups.
Age of Marriage	• Average age will rise as more first unions are consensual and older couples remarry.
	• The age will remain higher for males and higher-income groups.
Marriage Rate	• The rate will decline with more consensual unions.
	• It will remain higher for non-Christian religious groups and fundamentalist Christians.
Fertility Rate	• Fertility will continue to decline for younger and more educated women.
	• It will remain higher for low-income groups and certain cultural minorities.
Duration of Marriage	• Length of marriage will decline with the normalization and legitimation of divorce and more focus on self-development.
	• But older remarriages will remain more stable.
Re-partnering and Remarriage Rate	• Remarriage will rise as more people divorce but higher cohabitation rates mean reduced legal remarriage.
	• Non-legal re-partnering will be higher among low-income groups and divorced people.
Housework and Child Care	• More employed couples will hire home-cleaners and child-minders.
	• Women will continue to take responsibility for most indoor tasks, child care, and elder care.
	• Fathers will do more cooking, shopping, and child care but will retain responsibility for household and car repairs.
Labour Force Participation	• More mothers will work full-time and increase their contributions to household finances.
	• More fathers will work overtime or at two jobs.
	• Many parents will work longer hours to support their children, while others will experience unemployment or under-employment.

more security-conscious and choose to legalize their intimate relationships in an attempt to protect their assets. With less job security, rates of separation and divorce might also decline as fewer people will be able to afford two dwellings.

As both men and women pursue busy careers and older people seek new partners, more individuals will rely on introductions by friends, dating agencies, self-advertising in newspapers and on the Internet, and organized activities in order to find partners. Many of these relationships will become sexual soon after the individuals meet and some will lead to cohabitation without much consideration about permanence. Young people pursuing higher education will continue to live with their parents until they are well into their 20s, but when they leave the family home many will need to share accommodation as housing costs rise relative to income, especially in the major cities. This means that more young people will live with various room-mates and sexual partners but will not necessarily 'settle down' with one partner until they complete their education, develop some work stability, repay their debts, and acquire financial assets.

It also seems realistic to suggest that in the coming decades fewer adults will be living with relatives such as parents and siblings, but more will be creating non-traditional households based on neither the nuclear nor the extended family models. Also, more adults will avoid legal marriage in the future as sexuality becomes even more separated from marriage and reproduction, and men and women can more easily live—both socially and financially—without a legal partner. However, the social pressure to marry and to reproduce will remain strong. Most people will either cohabit or marry at least once in their life, as shared living provides greater opportunities for love, regular sex, and companionship while reducing loneliness and accommodation expenses. Considering current rates of separation, however, more people will cohabit with several consecutive partners over their lifetime but spend time 'between relationships' with casual intimacies, room-mates, living alone, or sharing a home with their children.

Judging from current trends in some European countries as well as in North America, a growing minority of intimate couples will 'live apart together' for specific periods of time while they study or work in separate locations. This will be especially prevalent among university-educated couples where overseas training and work are expected to bring higher occupational returns and where two high-level business or professional jobs are difficult to find in the same place. However, it will also remain a prevalent pattern for migrant couples, where one partner returns periodically to work or to oversee family business in their country of origin. Commuting couples might live together on the weekend or even less frequently but will be free to devote considerable amounts of time and energy to paid work or other activities when they are apart. This 'choice' will be influenced by higher rates of unemployment or under-employment, more international migration, and the growing importance of financial security for both men and women in a globalizing economy and during a world-wide economic recession.

Same-sex couples sharing a home will become more prevalent in the future, and more will live openly and choose to legalize their personal commitment. The legalization of same-sex relationships through 'civil union' legislation or the extension of marriage rights has already occurred in some jurisdictions and is under discussion in others. However, not all same-sex couples will choose to live in 'marriage-like relationships'. Gay men, especially, will be more likely than lesbian women to opt for a series of sexual partners while living alone close to a community of like-minded friends, or will choose to cohabit for short periods without any expectation of a lifelong partnership.

If a higher percentage of the population lives outside nuclear families, lifestyle and housing preferences will change as more people choose low-maintenance apartments or flats rather than single-family houses with gardens. With fewer family responsibilities and less household maintenance work, these people will likely spend less time at home and more time eating out, enjoying time with friends, attending leisure events, and travelling. These individuals and couples will be more likely to work full-time and overtime, to earn higher incomes, to spend less on home ownership and child-related expenses, and therefore to have more discretionary income for entertainment, recreation, and travel.

Generally, relationships will become more consensual and less permanent, although most people will continue to marry and produce children and grand-children. Giddens (1992) talked about the possibility of 'pure relationships' that would be unclouded by feelings of obligations, dependencies, and inequalities. Although this may be possible for some people, most couples will still depend on each other for financial support or domestic chores. Although more wives will earn household money, economic dependencies will continue as two incomes become essential to pay the household bills. In addition, economic inequalities and power differentials will continue between husbands and wives, reflecting gender inequalities in paid and unpaid work, including the responsibility for housework and the daily care of children. The probability of a 'pure relation-ship' could increase as more women become economically self-supporting, fewer children are born, and more fathers actively engage in child care. How-ever, most couples will marry and produce at least one child, and more mothers than fathers will become economically dependent on their partners.

As women expect more control over their lives, they will be more likely to initiate sexual and cohabiting relationships. However, vestiges of the double standard of sexuality will linger, penalizing women—through social stigma-tization and the possible negative impact on prospects for marriage and job promotion—who appear to be too obvious in their sexual needs or who openly admit that they are seeking recreational sex. With more consensual unions and liberal divorce laws, relationships will also last for shorter periods of time but people will be seeking new partners throughout the lifespan. Current patterns suggest that men will continue to prefer women who are attractive, 'petite', and unencumbered with children at home, and the age gap will become larger as older men seek new younger partners. Most children will continue to live with their mothers after separation, but these mothers will be expected to com-bine paid work and caring obligations, managing on lower female earnings. Although more women are gaining higher education and are working full-time,

Will Couples Stay Together?

Separation and divorce have become normalized and legitimized as they grow more prevalent, but the rising insecurity of intimate relationships will become more consequential in the future. First, the insecurity of legal marriage could discourage some young people from making public commitments because they will be afraid that their relationships might end in divorce, which could be legally complex, costly, and stigmatizing. Yet statistically, cohabiting relationships have higher rates of separation than legal marriages, suggesting that relationship instability will continue to increase at a societal level (Wu, 2000; Lichter and Quian, 2008).

Second, relationship instability will discourage young girls from accepting the idea that they can rely in the future on a male breadwinner and will encourage them to prepare for a lifetime of personal earning. More job-oriented education and career planning will reduce the gendered nature of paid work, raise the earnings of women relative to men, and increase wives' incomes relative to those of their husbands. However, the pattern for women to marry older men with higher incomes will also continue. Furthermore, by becoming more financially independent, women will also increase their chances of relationship instability because women who are self-supporting tend to feel less obliged to stay in unhappy relationships. Not only do they have fewer economic reasons to stay, but their male partners may also feel less guilt about separating from women who are self-supporting or who easily could become so.

More children will experience the dissolution of parental relationships, and when their parents are between partners, some children will begin to normalize living with one parent (usually the mother). If the mother re-partners, the children may initially feel some personal disruption but more children will view living in mother-led households and stepfamilies as normal. The boundaries of children's families will become more complex in stepfamilies, including both resident and non-resident parents and their new partners and parents, as well as step-siblings and grandparents from several relationships. Adapting to this complexity will undoubtedly challenge some children (and parents), but it will not necessarily lead to serious problems for them. Children will learn to become more flexible about their parents' intimate relationships, but parents and step-parents will also need to remain sensitive to children's perceptions and needs. No child or adolescent wants to feel displaced by her or his parent's new lover or new step-siblings, and more parents will be required to work at creating social cohesion within step-families or blended families.

If more adults re-partner later in life, the average age in all marriages will rise, dynamics will change in many families, and images of middle age and aging will gradually be refashioned. For many older couples, their new intimate relationships will provide a new lease on life, altering daily routines and prevalent images of sexuality, maturity, and parental obligations. The fact that some of the same transitions experienced by parents could simultaneously be happening to their mature children might help to bridge the generation gap even though the years between generations will be growing longer.

Will Aging Be a Problem?

Many demographers and politicians see the 'aging population' as a social problem and assume that more seniors in the population will burden society with higher pension and health-care costs. However, aging will not necessarily be a personal or family problem. Most older couples not only maintain high levels of independence but also provide services for friends and family, including lending money to their adult children and babysitting their grandchildren while the parents are working. In addition, many wives care for their husbands in their old age and some men care for their aging wives (Martin-Matthews, 2007; McDaniel, 2009). However, older unattached women are particularly vulnerable to poverty if they did not work for pay in their earlier years, if they suffer from health problems or disabilities, or if they did not own a home or inherit other assets.

Although life expectancy has been rising for centuries, some researchers now predict that it could begin to fall within the next two decades because of the high rates of obesity and its related diseases in developed countries such as Canada, the United States, and New Zealand (Walsh, 2005). Widespread obesity, especially among low-income people, will raise the already high rates of diabetes, heart disease, and strokes, as well as increase fertility problems. Researchers and policy-makers are particularly concerned about high rates of childhood obesity, which will undoubtedly cause future health problems and shorten lives. In addition, high rates of pollution and continued tobacco use are expected to reduce life expectancy in the future (ibid.).

As fertility declines and mothers are older when they produce their first child, the spacing between generations will become larger in the future. This may mean that fewer children will know their grandparents, although with higher living standards and improvements in health care some of their grandparents will live longer. These demographic changes also suggest that many parents will reach the former retirement age before their children reach maturity and leave home, forcing some parents to work longer to help finance their children's living and educational expenses. This could delay the retirement of more parents, which might provide an opportunity for governments to increase the eligibility age for retirement benefits in order to save public money.

Although governments often reform social programs to make them more consistent with current lifestyles, they also use changing family demography to justify forms of restructuring that save public money or downsize the welfare state. Studying family trends is therefore essential for governments. However, it is also useful to business people who are trying to predict or manipulate market trends for consumer products. For academics, studying patterns in intimate experiences and family life reveals the impact of the transformations occurring in the wider society and sheds light on the diversity and adaptability of human life.

The Future of Family Studies

Researchers and theorists have been studying family life for over a hundred years but the academic field of family studies, and especially the sociology of the family, has changed considerably over the decades. The field is certain to develop further in the future. While early research made false assumptions about the extent of uniformity, consensus, and cooperation within families, current research highlights diversity and conflict in family experiences. This includes a focus on gendered differences in domestic labour, power differentials in marriage, new patterns of family formation (including same-sex unions and cohabitation), cultural variations in marriage systems and family dynamics, and the impact of marital separation on various family members. Current studies also address the impact of politics, technology, and the media on the creation of 'personal biographies', new sexual practices, and cosmetic work on the body.

While social class was always a predominant variable in family research, gender, age, sexual preference, and **ethnicity** have also become central to current analyses of personal life and family practices. However, more studies continue to focus on young families with children rather than on families in mid-life. Women's family-related experiences have been researched more than men's but new studies on masculinity, fathering, and grandfathering are beginning to correct this imbalance (Mann, 2007). Particularly American and New Zealand research acknowledges the large differences in income, lifestyle, and family composition based on race, ethnicity, and culture. With higher rates of immigration and international travel, more researchers are focusing on cultural variations in marriage systems and family obligations, as well as the intergenerational differences between immigrants and their native-born children. The meaning of marriage and prevalent assumptions underlying family life are becoming especially relevant with immigration from Islamic and Hindu countries, as well as renewed interest in indigenous families. This indicates that the previous overemphasis on the Eurocentric, nuclear, and middle-class family is diminishing.

Despite this new focus, I argue in this book that social class continues to be a central variable influencing aspirations, achievements, and lifestyle. Studies with social policy implications continue to see household income and wealth accumulation as crucial variables influencing all aspects of personal life, although they seldom use the concept of social class. Many researchers continue to use the political economy approach to analyze the impact of global markets and social policy restructuring on family life. At the same time, new researchers tend to draw on the poststructuralist theoretical perspective, which gives primacy to the power of ideas and media representations. This approach, widely used in feminist analyses and cultural studies, emphasizes the importance of personal choice, identity, and consumerism, without always giving adequate consideration to the social and economic constraints on personal choices and identity creation.

In this book, I have used a theoretical perspective that I label the 'feminist political economy' approach because I focus on the impact of labour market and economic changes on gender relations. This approach reminds us that gendered patterns of work are promoted by current labour market practices but also that patterns of employment continue to shape the division of labour at home and the amount of time workers have to spend with their families. Working hours and conditions are modified by employers, unions, and governments, depending on their ideologies, political alliances, and power. However, the emphasis on the importance of paid work and the 'long-hours culture' is more prevalent in the liberal welfare states than in some European countries with shorter working hours, more holidays, and stronger support for parenting. We need to know more about the impact of working long hours on relations between spouses and between workers and their children. Future research could also help to understand how the new consumerism that accompanies **neo-liberalism** influences young people's aspirations for intimate relationships and future lifestyles.

The study of family patterns and intimate relationships has a long academic history, forming a significant portion of research and theorizing in sociology, anthropology, social work, gender studies, social psychology, and cultural studies. In recent years, researchers have been analyzing the impact of globalization and new efforts to restructure welfare states on employment patterns, on the growing gap between the rich and the poor, and on rising levels of household debt. However, social scientists are only beginning to explore the consequences of these economic transformations, as well as the impact of consumerism and advertising, on intimacy and family life.

Throughout this book I have argued that labour market constraints, increased migration, new technologies, and global ideas about equity and human rights are shaping intimate relationships. Although we may have acquired more choice to create our own personal biographies, we continue to live with some of the same socio-economic constraints, as well as several new limitations on our relationships.

Summary

Despite public concerns about the future of legal marriage and declining fertility rates, intimate relationships and child-bearing remain popular. However, more couples are marrying at later ages and fewer are producing large families because they believe that large families may jeopardize their opportunities and financial security. Current research in family studies focuses on cultural diversity, same-sex marriage, men's family experiences, and the growing impermanence of intimate relationships.

Questions for Critical Thought

1. Is there a future for legal marriage, considering that so many young couples now cohabit?

2. As more women work full-time and overtime, will household work be shared more equitably between male and female partners?

3. Will a deepening recession encourage more couples to legally marry and to stay together?

Suggested Readings

Beck-Gernsheim, Elisabeth. 2002. *Reinventing the Family: In Search of New Lifestyles*. Cambridge: Polity Press. This book discusses recent changes in family life, analyzes concerns about loss of stability, and argues that new forms of family life are expanding choices and opportunities.

Lewis, Jane. 2003. *Should We Worry About Family Change?* Toronto: University of Toronto Press. This book discusses the main policy debates about the family, outlining current socio-demographic changes and different views about how they should be interpreted.

Suggested Websites

The Future Families Project *www.vifamily.ca*
    The *Future Families Project: A Survey of Canadian Hopes and Dreams* by Reginald Bibby (2004) is discussed on the website of the Vanier Institute of the Family.

Glossary

Abuse   Deliberate maltreatment of another person that could be verbal, emotional, physical, or sexual.

Access   The legal arrangement for contact between a non-custodial parent and his/her offspring following separation or divorce.

Alimony   Spousal support awarded to divorced women before the enactment of no-fault divorce legislation.

Arranged marriage   A marriage in which the partner is selected by elder family members but the young people may have the right to veto the choice.

At-risk families   Families with a high probability of going hungry, having inadequate accommodation, or in which the likelihood of abusive behaviour is higher than normal.

Bilateral descent   Lineage traced through the families of both the bride and groom.

Blended families   Stepfamilies formed through post-marital cohabitation or remarriage that include step-siblings, half-siblings, or both.

Census family   A term used by Statistics Canada to refer to a married or cohabiting couple living with or without never-married children, and a lone parent living with never-married children.

Child custody   The guardianship of a child and the authority to make decisions about the child's welfare and upbringing.

Child poverty   The percentage of children living with impoverished parents, a concept designed to enhance sympathy for the plight of blameless children.

Child support   The privately arranged or court-ordered financial support a non-custodial parent must pay to support his/her offspring.

Civil code   Law, as in Quebec and many European countries, based largely on written statutes rather than previous court cases or custom (like common law).

Civil union   Marriage approved by the state but not necessarily by the church.

Cohabitation   An intimate union between a couple who share a household and live together in marriage-like circumstances; also called common-law marriage.

Cohort   A category of people either born at the same time or experiencing certain life stages or events at the same time.

Common law   The body of general, largely unwritten legal conventions based on prior judicial rulings and traditional customs.

Common-law relationships   Cohabitation without legal marriage.

Complementary roles   Separate spheres for men and women in marriage.

Conflict   Non-violent or violent disagreements or arguments within a relationship.

Corporatist welfare states   States whose social security is based on social insurance programs funded by employers, employees, and government, with higher benefits for those with higher incomes.

Developmental theory   Learning theory that assumes that children pass through stages of cognitive, motor, and psychological development, and that particular tasks or concepts must be adequately learned before a child passes through the next stage of development.

Divorce rates   The annual number of divorces per 1,000 marriages (or per 1,000 population) within a specific jurisdiction, such as a country or province.

Double standard   The differential evaluation for men and women of identical situations and behaviours.

Endogamy   Marriage within one's group, which may be race, ethnicity, religion, caste, or socio-economic status.

Ethnicity   Process of shared awareness of ancestral differences and group belonging used as a basis for differential distribution of recognition, rewards, and relationships.

Exchange theory   Application of a market analogy to explain attraction and commitment, assuming that individuals maximize rewards and minimize costs in intimate relationships just as they are assumed to in classic liberal economic theory.

Exogamy   Marriage outside the group.

Extended family   Several generations, or siblings and their spouses and children, who share a household and resources.

Family economy   The waged and unwaged contributions of all family members to ensuring the survival of the household.

Family policy   The pursuit and attainment of collective goals and values in addressing problems of families in relation to the state.

Family preservation   A principle governing child welfare that relies on the extended family and social support to keep children living with family members rather than placing them in foster homes or institutions.

Family values   Beliefs and attitudes that emphasize the (patriarchal) nuclear family as the basic unit of society and the importance of raising children.

Family wage   A single wage, normally earned by a breadwinner father, sufficient to support the entire family, hence avoiding the need for the paid labour of the wife or children.

Feminist perspective   An analytical framework focused on women's viewpoint and experiences, as well as on how social structures and cultural understandings impact on women.

First default principle   The state begins to enforce child support only if the parent fails to make the necessary payments.

Gendered roles   The ways that males and females interact in a society, considering their different socialization and life experiences.

Gender-neutral   Something that could pertain equally to male or female.

Generation   The time between the birth of a mother and her offspring, now about 30–35 years.

Globalization   The world scale of economic and other activity made possible by the spread of information and telecommunications technology, as well as improved and relatively low-cost transportation.

Homogamy   The similarities in the age, social class, race, and ethnicity of couples.

Incest taboos   These rules prevent couples from marrying or reproducing with those who are too closely related due to concerns about inbreeding, congenital abnormalities, and family jealously.

Industrialization   The process by which manufacturing industries become dominant in a country's economy.

In vitro fertilization   The union of sperm and egg outside a human being, typically in a test tube.

Joint custody   The legal situation where both parents share authority over decisions regarding child welfare and upbringing after divorce.

Kinship care   Alternative care by grandparents or other relatives instead of foster care by strangers.

Labour force   Those who are either engaged in formal paid employment or seeking paid employment.

Liberal welfare states   States in which social security is based largely on need and benefits are targeted to low-income and 'problem' families.

Lone-parent household   One parent sharing a residence with his or her never-married children.

Male breadwinner family   A two-parent family with the father as principal earner and the mother as care provider.

Marital breakdown   The legal grounds for divorce based on circumstances that impair marital functioning, such as spousal desertion or long-term separation.

Marriage market   A term that applies an economic analogy to describe the availability of potential marriage partners and how they are valued in a particular culture or period.

Maternity leave   The official time away from paid employment taken by a mother for childbirth or adoption.

Matriarchy   A system that gives women more authority than men.

Matrifocal family   A family focused around the mother.

Matrilineal descent   Tracing relatives through the mother's side of the family.

Matrilocal residence   The custom of the groom living with the bride's family or in her community.

Matrimonial fault   An act considered to violate the marriage contract and therefore to be a justification for divorce.

Medicalization of childbirth   The tendency to involve doctors, technological monitoring, and other medical interventions in childbirth.

Monogamy   A system of marriage in which each adult is allowed only one spouse at a time.

Monolithic bias   Assumption that all families are similar, with an overemphasis on uniformity of experience and structure at the expense of diversity.

Neo-liberalism   Political rationality that supports the restructuring of societies to better meet the demands of a global market economy, emphasizing competition, individual self-enhancement, and personal responsibility for problems.

Neo-local residence   The custom of the bride and groom living in a separate location from both of their birth families.

No-fault divorce   The legal provision for marital dissolution through a non-acrimonious process, as opposed to fault-based divorce that involves proving a spouse guilty of a matrimonial offence or fault.

Nuclear family   A husband and wife and their children sharing the same household and cooperating economically.

Parental leave   Official time away from paid employment that may be taken by either the mother or father at childbirth or adoption.

Patriarchy   Social or family system giving men more authority than women.

Patrilineal descent Lineage or family relationships traced through the male side of the family.

Patrilocal residence The bride moves into or near her husband's family home.

Political economy perspective Analytical approach emphasizing the links among economic changes, the work people do, policy decisions, and personal life.

Polyandry A system of marriage in which women are allowed more than one husband at a time.

Polygamy A system of marriage in which adults are allowed more than one spouse at a time.

Polygyny A system of marriage in which men are allowed more than one wife at a time.

Post-structuralism Theoretical perspective that explains social change through personal choices, the power of ideas, and public discourse rather than laws, rules, or access to power and money.

Power of the purse Theory that the person who earns most of the money controls the relationship or has greater decision-making power.

Psychoanalytic theory An approach to socialization that stresses the importance of early childhood experiences and subconscious emotions in shaping personality.

Re-partnering The transition into cohabitation or remarriage after divorce or separation.

Restructuring Organizational changes in workplaces to increase efficiency and save costs, usually involving layoffs.

Role models Persons whose behaviour is patterned by others.

Roles Patterns of behaviour governed by social expectations, rights, and duties, and associated with a specific position in a social situation (such as a husband in a family).

Same-sex marriage Gay and lesbian marriage.

Secularization The process of becoming less constrained by religious writings or authorities, or involving the separation of church and state.

Serial monogamy Marriage to one partner at a time but several over a lifetime.

Service sector The part of the economy that provides services rather than goods.

Shared parenting Both parents share the physical care and decision-making regarding the child during marriage or after divorce, regardless of who has legal custody.

Social class A category of people who share a similar social and economic position, and are conscious of their similarities.

Social constructionism A theoretical framework that argues that social reality and meaningful behaviour is created through social interaction and cultural understandings.

Social democratic welfare states States that seek to prevent poverty and inequality by providing state services and income support for everyone, regardless of family income.

Social exchange theory Use of economic analogies from cost–benefit analysis to explain marriage and family relations, which are assumed to involve a process of negotiation and the assessment of time/emotional investments.

Social institution An established set of roles, norms, and relationships organized around some central activity or social need.

Social insurance The pooling of the risk of unemployment, disability, or sickness among employers, employees/citizens, and the state, financed through contributions from all three groups.

Social learning theory The view that development occurs when children process social and cultural information from their environment by observing others, interpreting what they see, and then acting.

Socialization　The complex learning process through which individuals develop their personality and acquire the knowledge, skills, and motivation necessary for participation in social life.

State　The government as well as the public agencies that support and enforce its policies.

Structural functionalism　An analytical approach focusing on how social structure influences individual behaviour and assuming that behaviour is governed by rules, laws, and expectations that maintain the structure of society.

Surrogate mothers　Women who gestate and give birth to a child for another couple.

Survey research　Questionnaire-based collection of a large sample of quantitative data.

Symbolic interaction perspective　An analytical approach that assumes people create their own social reality by defining and interpreting the symbolic meanings of those responding to them.

Systems theory　An analytical perspective that sees the family as a system of interactions and relationships in which the behaviour of one member influences all others and behavioural patterns recur.

Telework　Work (often at home) through telecommunication or computer links to the main workplace.

Violence　Unwarranted physical or verbal force, or sexual aggression against another person.

Welfare state　The laws and social programs designed to protect citizens in times of unemployment, illness, old age, or insufficient income.

Bosch, Xavier. 1998. 'Spanish Doctors Criticised for High Tech Births', *British Medical Journal* 317, 7170 (21 Nov.): 1406.

Bowlby, J. 1953. 'Some Pathological Processes Set in Train by Early Mother-Child Separation', *Journal of Mental Science* 99: 265–72.

———. 1958. 'The Nature of the Child's Tie to His Mother', *International Journal of Psycho-Analysis* 39: 350–73.

———. 1969. *Attachment*. New York: Basic Books.

Boyd, Susan B. 2003. *Child Custody, Law, and Women's Work*. Toronto: Oxford University Press.

Bradbury, Bettina. 2005. 'Social, Economic, and Cultural Origins of Contemporary Families', in Baker (2005a): 71–98.

Bradbury, Bruce, and Kate Norris. 2005. 'Income and Separation', *Journal of Sociology* 41, 4 (Dec.): 425–46.

Braithwaite, Dawn O., and Leslie A. Baxter. 2005. *Engaging Theories in Family Communication: Multiple Perspectives*. Sage.

Brennan, Deborah. 1998. *The Politics of Australian Child Care: Philanthropy, Feminism and Beyond*. Melbourne: Cambridge University Press.

———. 2007a. 'Babies, Budgets, and Birthrates: Work/Family Policy in Australia 1996–2006', *Social Politics* (Spring): 31–57.

———. 2007b. 'The ABC of Child Care Politics', *The Australian Journal of Social Issues* 42, 2 (Winter): 213–25.

Broude, G. 1994. *Marriage, Family, and Relationships*. Denver: ABCCLIO.

Brown, Judith. 1988. 'Iroquois Women: An Ethnohistoric Note', in B. Fox, ed., *Family Bonds and Gender Relations*. Toronto: Canadian Scholars' Press, 83–98.

Brownridge, Douglas A. 2003. 'Male Partner Violence against Aboriginal Women in Canada: An Empirical Analysis', *Journal of Interpersonal Violence* 18: 65–83.

———. 2008. 'The Elevated Risk for Violence Against Cohabiting Women: A Comparison of Three Nationally Representative Surveys of Canada', *Violence Against Women* 14, 7: 809–32.

Bulbeck, Chilla. 2005. '"Women are Exploited Way Too Often": Feminist Rhetorics at the End of Equality', *Australian Feminist Studies* 20, 46 (Mar.): 71–2.

Burghes, L. 1994. *Lone Parenthood and Family Disruption*. Occasional Paper #18. London: Family Policy Studies Centre.

Butler, Judith. 1997. *The Psychic Life of Power: Theories of Subjection*. Stanford, Calif.: Stanford University Press.

Callan, Victor J. 1982. 'How Do Australians Value Children? A Review and Research Update Using the Perceptions of Parents and Voluntarily Childless Adults', *Australian and New Zealand Journal of Sociology* 18, 3: 384–98.

Cameron, Jan. 1990. *Why Have Children? A New Zealand Case Study*. Christchurch: Canterbury University Press.

———. 1997. *Without Issue: New Zealanders Who Choose Not to Have Children*. Christchurch: Canterbury University Press.

Canada, Department of Justice. 2003. 'Child Support', available at http://canada.justice. gc.ca/en/ps/sup/index.html.

Canadian Institute of Child Health. 2002. *The Health of Canada's Children*, 3rd edn. Ottawa: Canadian Institute of Child Health.

Caro, Francis G. ed. 2006. *Family and Aging Policy*. London: The Haworth Press.

Cartwright, Claire. 2006. 'You Want to Know How It Affected Me? Young Adults' Perceptions of the Impact of Parental Divorce', *Journal of Divorce and Remarriage* 44, 3/4: 125–43.

————, and Heather McDowell. 2008. 'Young Women's Life Stories and Accounts of Parental Divorce', *Journal of Divorce and Remarriage* 49, 1/2: 56–77.

Castles, Francis G. 1985. *The Working Class and Welfare: Reflections on the Political Development of the Welfare State in Australia and New Zealand, 1890–1980*. Sydney: Allen & Unwin.

————. 2002. 'Three Facts about Fertility: Cross-National Lessons for the Current Debate', *Family Matters* 63 (Spring/Summer): 22–7.

————, and Ian F. Shirley. 1996. 'Labour and Social Policy: Gravediggers or Refurbishers of the Welfare State?', in F. Castles, R. Gerritsen, and J. Vowles, eds, *The Great Experiment: Labour Parties and Public Policy Transformation in Australia and New Zealand*. Auckland: Auckland University Press, 88–106.

Cates, Norman. 1993. 'Trends in Care and Services for Elderly Individuals in Denmark and Sweden', *International Journal of Aging and Human Development* 37, 4: 271–6.

Cavanagh, Shannon E. 2008. 'Family Structure History and Adolescent Adjustment', *Journal of Family Issues* 29, 7: 944–80.

Cheal, David. 1991. *Family and the State of Theory*. Toronto: University of Toronto Press.

————. 1996. 'Stories about Step-families', in *Growing Up In Canada: National Longitudinal Survey of Children and Youth*. Ottawa: Human Resources Development Canada and Statistics Canada, 93–101.

Che-Alford, Janet, and Brian Hamm. 1999. 'Under One Roof: Three Generations Living Together', *Canadian Social Trends* 53 (Summer): 6–9.

Cherlin, Andrew J. 1996. *Public and Private Families: An Introduction*. New York: McGraw-Hill.

Cherniak, Donna, and Jane Fisher. 2008. 'Explaining Obstetric Interventionism: Technical Skills, Common Conceptualisations, or Collective Countertransferance?' *Women's Studies International Forum* 31: 270–7.

Chesnais, J.C. 1992. *The Demographic Transition: Stages, Patterns, and Economic Implications*. Oxford: Clarendon Press.

Cheyne, Christine, Mike O'Brien, and Michael Belgrave. 2008. *Social Policy in Aotearoa New Zealand*, 4th edn. Melbourne: Oxford University Press.

Childcare Resource and Research Unit, University of Toronto (CRRU). 2003. 'Childcare in the News' (online), 11 Dec.

Chodorow, Nancy. 1978. *The Reproduction of Mothering: Psychoanalysis and the Sociology of Gender*. Berkeley, Calif.: University of California Press.

————. 1989. *Feminism and Psychoanalytic Theory*. New Haven: Yale University Press.

Christopher, K., P. England, S. McLanahan, K. Ross, and T.M. Smeeding. 2001. 'Gender Inequality in Affluent Nations: The Role of Single Motherhood and the State', in K. Vleminckx and T.M. Smeeding, eds, *Child Wellbeing, Child Poverty and Child Policy in Modern Nations*. Bristol: Policy Press, 199–220.

Clark, Warren. 2006. 'Interreligious Unions in Canada', Ottawa: Statistics Canada, available at http://www.statcan.ca/english/freepub/11–008-XIE/2006003/tables/interreligious_table.

Clements, M., A. Cordova, H. Markman, and J. Laurenceau. 1997. 'The Erosion of Marital Satisfaction Over Time and How to Prevent It', in R.J. Stern and M. Hojjat, eds, *Satisfaction in Close Relationships*. New York: Guilford Press.

Cockett, M., and J. Tripp. 1994. *The Exeter Family Study*. Exeter, UK: University of Exeter.

Collins, Simon. 2005. 'Sperm Donors Could Become "Third Parents"', *New Zealand Herald*, 21 Apr., A3.

Coltrane, Scott. 1998. *Gender and Families*. Thousand Oaks, Calif.: Pine Forge Press.

Connidis, Ingrid. 2009. *Family Ties and Aging*, 2nd edn. Thousand Oaks, Calif.: Pine Forge Press.

Connolly, Ellen. 2004. 'You've Come Almost No Distance At All, Baby', *Sydney Morning Herald*, 15 Dec. (online).

Connolly, Marie. 2003. 'Kinship Care—A Selected Literature Review', unpublished paper prepared for the Department of Child Youth and Family Services, Wellington, NZ.

Cooley, Charles H. 1902. *Human Nature and Social Order*. New York: Charles Scribner's Sons.

Correll, S., S. Benard, and I. Paik. 2007. 'Getting a Job: Is there a Motherhood Penalty?' *American Journal of Sociology* 112, 5: 1297–338.

Coveney, Peter. 1982. 'The Image of the Child', in C. Jenks, ed., *The Sociology of Childhood*. London: Batsford, 42–7.

Cowan, Carolyn, et al. 1985. 'Transition to Parenthood: His, Hers, and Theirs', *Journal of Family Issues* 6: 451–81.

Craig, Lyn. 2006. 'Parental Education, Time in Paid Work and Time with Children: An Australian Time-Diary Analysis', *British Journal of Sociology* 57, 4: 553–75.

———, and Michael Bittman. 2008. 'The Incremental Time Costs of Children: An Analysis of Children's Impact on Adult Time Use in Australia', *Feminist Economics* 14, 2 (April): 59–88.

Crittenden, A. 2001. *The Price of Motherhood: Why the Most Important Job in the World is Still the Least Valued*. New York: Metropolitan Books.

Crompton, Rosemary. 2004. 'Women's Employment and Work/Life Balance in Britain and Europe', plenary address at conference 'Work/Life Balance across the Life Course', University of Edinburgh, 1 July.

Crouter, Ann C., and Alan Booth. 2006. *Romance and Sex in Adolescence and Emerging Adulthood: Risks and Opportunities*. New York/London: Routledge.

Cuneo, Carl. 1979. 'State, Class and Reserve Labour: The Case of the 1941 Unemployment Insurance Act', *Canadian Review of Sociology and Anthropology* 16, 2: 147–70.

Cunningham, Mick, and Arland Thornton. 2006. 'The Influence of Parents' Marital Quality on Adult Children's Attitudes toward Marriage and Its Alternatives: Main and Moderating Effects', *Demography* 43, 4: 659–72.

Curtis, Lori J. 2001. 'Lone Motherhood and Health Status', *Canadian Public Policy* 27, 3: 335–56.

Dalley, Bronwyn. 1998. *Family Matters: Child Welfare in Twentieth Century New Zealand*. Auckland: Auckland University Press.

Davis, S.N., T.N. Greenstein, and J.P. Marks. 2007. 'Effects of Union Type on Division of Household Labor', *Journal of Family Issues* 28, 9: 1246–72.

DeKeseredy, Walter. 2005. 'Patterns of Family Violence', in Baker (2005a: 229–57).

Dempsey, Ken. 1997. *Inequalities in Work and Marriage: Australia and Beyond*. Melbourne: Oxford University Press.

——, and David De Vaus. 2004. 'Who Cohabits in 2001? The Significance of Age, Gender and Religion', *Journal of Sociology* 40, 2: 157–78.

De Vaus, David. 2002. 'Marriage and Mental Health', *Family Matters* 62 (Winter): 26–32.

Devereux, Monique. 2004. 'Religious Leaders Say Wearing Veils Is a Personal Choice', *New Zealand Herald*, 2 Nov., available at http://www.nzherald.co.nz.

Dewson, Emma. 2004. 'Off to the Dance: Romance in Rural New Zealand Communities, 1880s–1920s', *History Australia* 2, 1 (December).

Dickason, Olive Patricia. 2006. *A Concise History of Canada's First Nations*. Toronto: Oxford University Press.

Doodson, Lisa, and David Morley. 2006. 'Understanding the Roles of Non-Residential Step-mothers', *Journal of Divorce and Remarriage* 45, 3/4: 109–30

Dorsett, Richard, and Alan Marsh. 1998. *The Health Trap: Poverty, Smoking and Lone Parenthood*. London: Policy Studies Institute.

Doucet, Andrea. 2006. *Do Men Mother?* Toronto: University of Toronto Press.

Douthitt, Robin A., and Joanne Fedyk. 1990. *The Cost of Raising Children in Canada*. Toronto: Butterworths.

Doyal, L. 1995. *What Makes Women Sick? Gender and the Political Economy of Health*. New Brunswick, NJ: Rutgers University Press.

Dranoff, Linda Silver. 1977. *Women in Canadian Life*. Toronto: Fitzhenry & Whiteside.

Drolet, Marie, and René Morissette. 1997. 'Working More? What Do Workers Prefer?' *Perspectives on Labour and Income* 9, 4: 32–8.

Dumas, Jean, and Yves Péron. 1992. *Marriage and Conjugal Life in Canada*. Ottawa: Statistics Canada (Catalogue no. 91–534E).

Dunne, G. 2000. 'Opting into Motherhood: Lesbians Blurring the Boundaries and Transforming the Meaning of Parenthood and Kinship', *Gender and Society* 14: 11–35.

Dwyer, Angela E. 2006. 'From Private to Public Bodies: Normalising Pregnant Bodies in Western Culture', *Nexus: Newsletter of The Australian Sociological Association* 18, 3: 18–19.

Dykstra, Pearl A. 2006. 'Off the Beaten Track: Childlessness and Social Integration in Later Life', *Research on Aging* 28: 749–67.

Dykstra, P., and T. Fokkema. 2007. 'Social and Emotional Loneliness Among Divorced and Married Men and Women: Comparing the Deficit and Cognitive Perspectives', *Basic and Applied Social Psychology* 29, 1: 1–12.

Edin, Kathryn. 2003. 'Work Is Not Enough', plenary address to Australian Social Policy Conference, University of New South Wales, Sydney, 10 July.

——, and Maria J. Kefalas. 2005. *Promises I Can Keep: Why Poor Women Put Motherhood before Marriage*. Berkeley: University of California Press.

——, and Laura Lein. 1997. *Making Ends Meet: How Single Mothers Survive Welfare and Low-Wage Work*. New York: Russell Sage Foundation.

——, and Joanna M. Reed. 2005. 'Why Don't They Just Get Married? Barriers to Marriage among the Disadvantaged', *Marriage and Child Wellbeing* 15, 2: 117–36.

Edlund, Jonas. 2007. 'The Work–Family Time Squeeze: Conflicting Demands of Paid and Unpaid Work among Working Couples in 29 Countries', *International Journal of Comparative Sociology* 48, 6: 451–80.

Edwards, Anne, and Susan Magarey, eds. 1995. *Women in a Restructuring Australia: Work and Welfare*. Sydney: Allen & Unwin.

Eichler, Margrit. 1988. *Families in Canada Today*, 2nd edn. Toronto: Gage.

———. 1997. *Family Shifts: Families, Policies, and Gender Equality*. Toronto: Oxford University Press.

———. 2005. 'Biases in Family Literature', Baker (2005a): 52–68.

Eichler, Margrit, Patrizia Albanese, Susan Ferguson, Nicky Hyndman, Lichun Willa Liu, and Ann Matthews. *More Than it Seems: Household Work and Lifelong Learning*. Toronto: Canadian Scholars' Press.

Elizabeth, Vivienne. 2000. 'Cohabitation, Marriage, and the Unruly Consequences of "Difference"', *Gender and Society* 14, 1: 87–100.

———. 2001. 'Managing Money, Managing Coupledom: A Critical Investigation of Cohabitants' Money Management Practices', *Sociological Review* 49: 389–411.

Elizabeth, Vivienne, and Wendy Larner. 2009. 'Racializing the "Social Development" State: Investing in Children in Aortearoa New Zealand', *Social Politics* 16, 1: 1–27.

Elliott, J., and M. Richards. 1991. 'Parental Divorce and the Life Chances of Children', *Family Law*: 481–4.

———, ———, and H. Warwick. 1993. *The Consequences of Divorce for the Health and Well-Being of Adults and Children*. Final Report for Health Promotion Trust #2. Cambridge, UK: Centre for Family Research.

Emery, R. 1994. 'Psychological Research on Children, Parents, and Divorce', in Emery, ed., *Renegotiating Family Relationships: Divorce, Child Custody, and Mediation*. New York: Guilford Press, 194–217.

Engels, Friedrich. 1972 [1884]. *The Origin of the Family, Private Property and the State*. New York: Pathfinder.

Erfani, Amir, and Roderic Beaujot. 2006. 'Familial Orientations and the Rationales for Childbearing Behaviour', *Canadian Studies in Population* 33, 1: 49–67.

Erikson, E. 1963. *Childhood and Society*, 2nd edn. New York: Norton.

———. 1968. *Identity: Youth and Crisis*. New York: Norton.

Ermisch, John. 1991. *Lone Parenthood: An Economic Analysis*. Cambridge: Cambridge University Press.

———. 2003. *An Economic Analysis of the Family*. Oxford: Princeton University Press.

Esping-Andersen, Gøsta. 1990. *The Three Worlds of Welfare Capitalism*. Cambridge: Polity Press.

———, ed. 1996. *Welfare States in Transition: National Adaptations in Global Economies*. London: Sage.

Evenson, Ranae, and Robin W. Simon. 2005. 'Clarifying the Relationship between Parenthood and Depression', *Journal of Health and Social Behaviour* 46: 341–58.

Evertsson, Marie. 2006. 'The Reproduction of Gender: Housework and Attitudes Toward Gender Equality in the Home Among Swedish boys and Girls', *British Journal of Sociology* 57, 3: 415–36.

Featherstone, M. 1991. 'The Body in Consumer Culture', in M. Featherstone and B.S. Turner, eds, *The Body: Social Process and Cultural Theory*. London: Sage.

Ferri, E. 1984. *Step Children: A National Study*. Windsor, UK: NFER-Nelson.

———, and K. Smith. 2003. 'Partnerships and Parenthood', in E. Ferri, J. Bynner, and M. Wadsmith, eds, *Changing Britain, Changing Lives*. London: Institute of Education.

Fisman, R., S. Iyengar, E. Kamenica, and I. Simonson. 2006. 'Gender Differences in Mate Selection: Evidence from a Speed Dating Experiment', *The Quarterly Journal of Economics* 121, 2: 673–97.

Fleising, Usher. 2003. 'Bride-Price', in Ponzetti (2003): 175–6.

Fleming, Robin. 1997. *The Common Purse*. Auckland: Auckland University Press.

———, with Toni Atkinson. 1999. *Families of a Different Kind*. Waikanae, NZ: Families of Remarriage Project.

———, and S.K. Easting. 1994. *Couples, Households and Women: Report of the Pakeha Component of the Intrafamily Income Study*, Wellington Intrafamily Income Project. Palmerston North, NZ: Social Policy Research Centre, Massey University.

Fletcher, G. 1978. 'Division of Labour in the New Zealand Nuclear Family', *New Zealand Psychologist* 7, 2: 33–40.

Fletcher, R. 1973. *The Family and Marriage in Britain*. Harmondsworth: Penguin.

Ford, Jane, Natasha Nassar, Elizabeth Sullivan, Georgina Chambers, and Paul Lancaster. 2003. *Reproductive Health Indicators, Australia, 2002*. Sydney: Australian Institute of Health and Welfare.

Fox, Bonnie. 2001. 'The Formative Years: How Parenthood Creates Gender', *Canadian Review of Sociology and Anthropology* 38, 4: 373–90.

———. 2006. 'Motherhood as a Class Act: The Many Ways in Which "Intensive Mothering" Is Entangled with Social Class', in Kate Bezanson and Meg Luxton, eds, *Social Reproduction: Feminist Political Economy Challenges Neo-Liberalism*. Montreal and Kingston: McGill-Queens University Press, 231–62.

Friedan, Betty. 1963. *The Feminine Mystique*. New York: Norton.

Friendly, Martha, and Jane Beach. 2005. *Early Childhood Education and Care in Canada*, 6th edn. Toronto: Childcare Resource and Research Unit.

Funder, Kathleen. 1996. *Remaking Families: Adaptation of Parents and Children to Divorce*. Melbourne: Australian Institute of Family Studies.

———, and Margaret Harrison. 1993. 'Drawing a Longbow on Marriage and Divorce', in K. Funder, M. Harrison, and R. Weston, eds, *Settling Down: Pathways of Parents after Divorce*. Melbourne: Australian Institute of Family Studies, 13–32.

Furstenberg, F., F. Morgan, and P. Allison. 1987. 'Paternal Participation and Children's Well-Being after Marital Dissolution', *American Sociological Review* 52: 695–701.

Gaffield, Chad. 1990. 'The Social and Economic Origins of contemporary Families', in M. Baker, ed., *Families: Changing Trends in Canada*, 2nd edn. Toronto: McGraw-Hill Ryerson, 23–40.

Gauthier, Anne Hélène. 1996. *The State and the Family: A Comparative Analysis of Family Policies in Industrialized Countries*. Oxford: Clarendon Press.

Gauthier, A. 2002. 'The Role of Grandparents', *Current Sociology* 50, 2: 295–307.

Gazso-Windle, Amber, and Julie Ann McMullin. 2003. 'Doing Domestic Labour: Strategising in a Gendered Domain', *Canadian Journal of Sociology* 28, 3: 341–66.

Gershuny, Jonathan, and Oriel Sullivan. 2003. 'Time Use, Gender, and Public Policy Regimes', *Social Politics* 10, 2: 205–28.

Giddens, Anthony. 1992. *The Transformation of Intimacy: Sexuality, Love and Eroticism in Modern Societies*. Cambridge: Polity Press.

———. 2006. *Sociology*, 5th edn. Cambridge: Polity Press.

Gilding, Michael. 1997. *Australian Families: A Comparative Perspective*. Melbourne: Addison Wesley Longman.

Leslie, Gerald, and Sheila K. Korman. 1989. *The Family in Social Context*, 7th edn. New York: Oxford University Press.

Letherby, G. 1999. 'Other than Mother and Mothers as Others: The Experience of Motherhood and Non-motherhood in Relation to "Infertility" and "Involuntary Childlessness"', *Women's Studies International Forum* 22: 359–72.

Lewis, Jane. 1992. 'Gender and the Development of Welfare State Regimes', *Journal of European Social Policy* 2, 3: 159–73.

———. 1999. 'Marriage and Cohabitation and the Nature of Commitment', *Child and Family Law Quarterly* 11, 4: 355–63.

———. 2003. *Should We Worry about Family Change?* Toronto: University of Toronto Press.

Lichter, D.T., and Z. Quian. 2008. 'Serial Cohabitation and the Marital Life Course', *Journal of Marriage and Family* 70, 4: 861–78.

———, ———, and L.M. Mellot. 2006. 'Marriage or Dissolution? Union Transitions among Poor Cohabiting Women', *Demography* 43, 2: 223–40.

Lindsay, Colin. 2008. 'Are Women Spending More Time on Unpaid Domestic Work than Men in Canada?', *Matter of Fact*. Statistics Canada, Catalogue 89–630 X.

Lipman, Ellen L., David R. Offord, and Martin D. Dooley. 1996. 'What Do We Know about Children from Single-Parent Families? Questions and Answers from the National Longitudinal Survey on Children', in *Growing Up in Canada: National Longitudinal Survey on Children and Youth*. Ottawa: Human Resources Development Canada.

Little, Margaret. 1998. *No Car, No Radio, No Liquor Permit: The Moral Regulation of Single Mothers in Ontario, 1920–1997*. Toronto: Oxford University Press.

Lopata, Helena. 1971. *Occupation: Housewife*. New York: Oxford University Press.

Lundberg, Shelly, and Elaina Rose. 1998. 'The Determinants of Specialization within Marriage', discussion paper, Department of Economics, University of Washington.

Lunt, Neil, Mike O'Brien, and Robert Stephens, eds. 2008. *New Zealand, New Welfare*. Auckland, NZ: CENGAGE Learning.

Lupri, Eugen, and James Frideres. 1981. 'The Quality of Marriage and the Passage of Time: Marital Satisfaction over the Family Life Cycle', *Canadian Journal of Sociology* 6, 3: 283–306.

Luxton, Meg. 1980. *More Than a Labour of Love*. Toronto: Women's Education Press.

———. 2009. 'Conceptualizing "Families": Theoretical Frameworks', in Baker (2005a).

———, and June Corman. 2001. *Getting By in Hard Times: Gendered Labour at Home and on the Job*. Toronto: University of Toronto Press.

McDaniel, Susan A. 2009. 'The Family Lives of the Middle-Aged and Elderly in Canada', in M. Baker, ed., *Families: Changing Trends in Canada*, 6th edn. Toronto: McGraw-Hill Ryerson, 225–42.

———, and Lorne Tepperman. 2000. *Close Relations: An Introduction to the Sociology of the Families*, 1st edn. Toronto: Pearson/Prentice-Hall.

———, and ———. 2004. *Close Relations: An Introduction to the Sociology of the Families*, 2nd edn. Toronto: Pearson/Prentice-Hall.

McDonald, Peter. 2000. 'Gender Equity in Theories of Fertility Transition', *Population and Development Review* 26, 3: 427–39.

McFadden, Suzanne. 2005. 'Teen Money: Get Real', *Canvas, Weekend Herald* (New Zealand), 9 Apr., 10–12.

McGillvray, A., and B. Comaskey. 1998. '"Everybody Has Black Eyes . . . Nobody Don't Say Nothing": Intimate Violence, Aboriginal Women, and the Justice System Response', in K.D. Bonnycastle and G.S. Rigakos, eds, *Unsettling Truths: Battered Women, Policy, Politics and Contemporary Research in Canada*. Vancouver: Collective Press.

McGilly, Frank. 1998. *An Introduction to Canada's Public Social Services: Understanding Income and Health Programs*, 2nd edn. Toronto: Oxford University Press.

McKay, S., and K. Rowlingson. 1998. 'Choosing Lone Parenthood? The Dynamics of Family Change', in R. Ford and J. Millar, eds, *Private Lives and Public Responses: Lone Parenthood and Future Policy in the UK*. London: Policy Studies Institute, 42–57.

McKenna, K., A. Green, and M. Gleason. 2002. 'Relationship Formation on the Internet: What's the Big Attraction?' *Journal of Social Issues* 58, 1: 9–31.

Mackey, R.A., and B.A. O'Brien. 1995. *Lasting Marriages: Men and Women Growing Together*. Westport, Conn.: Praeger.

McLaughlin, Diane K., and Daniel T. Lichter. 1997. 'Poverty and the Marital Behavior of Young Women', *Journal of Marriage and the Family* 59: 589.

Maclean, M., and D. Kuh. 1991. 'The Long Term Effects for Girls of Parental Divorce', in M. Maclean and D. Groves, eds, *Women's Issues in Social Policy*. London: Routledge, 161–78.

McMahon, A. 1999. *Taking Care of Men*. Cambridge: Cambridge University Press.

McNair, Ruth, Deborah Dempsey, Sarah Wise, and Amaryll Perlesz. 2002. 'Lesbian Parenting: Issues, Strengths and Challenges', *Family Matters* 63: 40–9.

Madsen, Stephanie D. 2008. 'Parents' Management of Adolescents' Romantic Relationships through Dating Rules: Gender Variations and Correlates of Relationship Qualities', *Journal of Youth and Adolescence* 37, 9: 1044–58.

Magarick, R.H., and R.A. Brown. 1981. 'Social and Emotional Aspects of Voluntary Childlessness in Vasectomized Childless Men', *Journal of Biosocial Science* 13: 157–67.

Malin, M., E. Hemminki, O. Raikkonen, S. Sihvo, and M. Perala. 2001. 'What Do Women Want? Women's Experiences of Infertility Treatment', *Social Science and Medicine* 53: 123–33.

Mann, Robin. 2007. 'Out of the Shadows?: Grandfatherhood, Age and Masculinities', *Journal of Aging Studies* 21: 281–91.

Marcil-Gratton, Nicole. 1998. *Growing Up with Mom and Dad? The Intricate Family Life Courses of Canadian Children*. Ottawa: Ministry of Industry.

Marshall, Katherine. 1993. 'Employed Parents and the Division of Labour', *Perspectives on Labour and Income* 5, 3: 23–30.

———. 1994. 'Balancing Work and Family Responsibilities', *Perspectives on Labour and Income* 6, 1: 26–30.

———. 1998. 'Stay-at-Home Dads', *Perspectives on Labour and Income* 10, 1: 9–15.

Martin, Chantal, and Paul Robinson. 2008. *Child and Spousal Support: Maintenance enforcement Survey Statistics, 2006/2007*. Catalogue #85–228-XIE. Statistics Canada: Ottawa: Ministry of Industry.

Martin-Matthews, Anne. 2007. 'Situating "Home" at the Nexus of the Public and Private Spheres', *Current Sociology* 55, 2: 229–49.

Mason, Jennifer, Vanessa May, and Lynda Clarke. 2007. 'Ambivalence and Paradoxes of Grandparenting', *The Sociological Review* 55, 4: 687–706.

May, Elaine Campbell. 1995. *Barren in the Promised Land: Childless Americans and the Pursuit of Happiness*. New York: Basic Books.

Mead, George H. 1934. *Mind, Self and Society*. Chicago: Chicago University Press.

Mead, Margaret. 1935. *Sex and Temperament in Three Primitive Societies*. New York: Dell.

Meezan, William, and Jonathan Rauch. 2005. 'Gay Marriage, Same-Sex Parenting, and America's Children', *Marriage and Family Well-being* 15, 2: 97–114.

Merla, Laura. 2008. 'Determinants, Costs, and Meanings of Stay-at-Home Fathers: An International Comparison', *Fathering: A Journal of Theory, Research and Practice about Men as Fathers* 6, 2 (Spring): 113–32.

Michaels, M.W. 1996. 'Other Mothers: Toward an Ethic of Postmaternal Practice', *Hypatia* 11, 2: 49–70.

Millar, Jane, and Karen Rowlingson, eds. 2001. *Lone Parents, Employment and Social Policy: Cross-National Comparisons*. Bristol: Policy Press.

———, and Peter Whiteford. 1993. 'Child Support in Lone-Parent Families: Policies in Australia and the UK', *Policy and Politics* 21, 1: 59–72.

Millett, Kate. 1970. *Sexual Politics*. New York: Doubleday.

MSD (Ministry of Social Development). 2008. *Children and Young People: Indicators of Well-being in New Zealand 2008*. Summary Table of Indicators, available at http://www.msd.govt.nz.

Mink, Gwendolyn. 1998. *Welfare's End*. Ithaca, NY: Cornell University Press.

———. 2002. 'Violating Women: Rights Abuses in the American Welfare Police State', in Sylvia Bashevkin, ed., *Women's Work Is Never Done*. New York: Routledge, 141–64.

Mitchell, Barbara A. 2007. *The Boomerang Age*. New Brunswick, NJ: Transaction Publishers.

Mitchell, Juliet. 1974. *Psychoanalysis and Feminism*. Harmondsworth: Penguin.

———, and Jack Goody. 1997. 'Feminism, Fatherhood and the Family in Britain', in Ann Oakley and Juliet Mitchell, eds, *Who's Afraid of Feminism? Seeing Through the Backlash*. London: Hamish Hamilton.

Monari, F., S. Di Mario, F. Facchinetti, and V. Basevi. 2008. 'Obstetritians' and Midwives' Attitudes toward Cesarean Section', *Birth* 35, 2 : 129–35.

Mongeau, P.A., and C.M. Carey. 1996. 'Who's Wooing Whom: An Experimental Investigation of Date Initiation and Expectancy Violation', *Western Journal of Communication* 60, 3: 195–213.

Montgomerie, Deborah. 1999. 'Sweethearts, Soldiers, Happy Families: Gender and the Second World War', in Caroline Daley, ed., *The Gendered Kiwi*. Auckland: Auckland University Press, 163–90.

Moore, Oliver. 2003. 'Bush Wants to "Codify" Heterosexual Unions', *Globe and Mail*, 31 July.

Morell, Carolyn M. 1994. *Unwomanly Conduct: The Challenges of Intentional Childlessness*. New York: Routledge.

Mullender, Audrey, G. Hague, U. Imam, L. Kelly, E. Malos, and L. Regan. 2003. 'Could Have Helped but Didn't: The Formal and Informal Support Systems Experienced by Children Living with Domestic Violence', in C. Hallett and A. Prout, eds, *Hearing the Voices of Children: Social Policy for a New Century*. London and New York: Routledge Falmer.

Murdock, George. 1949. *Social Structure*. New York: Macmillan.

Myles, John. 1996. 'When Markets Fail: Social Welfare in Canada and the United States', in Esping-Andersen (1996: 116–40).

Nanda, Serena, and Richard Warms. 2007. *Cultural Anthropology*, 9th edn. Belmont, Calif.: Wadsworth.

National Council of Welfare (NCW). 2008. *Welfare Incomes 2006 and 2007*. Ottawa: Minister of Public Works and Government Services Canada.

National Longitudinal Survey of Children and Youth (NLSCY). 1996. *Growing Up in Canada*. Ottawa: Human Resources Development Canada and Statistics Canada.

Neal, Margaret B. 2007. *Working Couples Caring for Children and Aging Parents: Effects of Work and Well-Being*. Mahwah, NJ: Erlbaum.

Nelson, E.D., and Barrie W. Robinson. 1999. *Gender in Canada*. Scarborough, Ont.: Prentice-Hall Allyn and Bacon Canada.

Nelson, F. 1996. *Lesbian Motherhood*. Toronto: University of Toronto Press.

———. 2001. 'Lesbian Families', in Bonnie J. Fox, ed., *Family Patterns, Gender Relations*, 2nd edn. Toronto: Oxford University Press.

Nett, Emily. 1981. 'Canadian Families in Social-Historical Perspective', *Canadian Journal of Sociology* 6, 3: 239–60.

———. 1993. *Canadian Families Past and Present*, 2nd edn. Toronto: Butterworths.

NZHRC (New Zealand Housing Research Centre). no date. 'Homeownership in New Zealand', Dunedin: University of Otago, available at http://www.otago.ac.nz.

Oakley, Ann. 1974. *The Sociology of Housework*. Oxford: Martin Robertson.

O'Connor, Julia S., Ann Shola Orloff, and Sheila Shaver. 1999. *States, Markets, Families: Gender Liberalism and Social Policy in Australia, Canada, Great Britain and the United States*. Cambridge: Cambridge University Press.

O'Leary, K.D., et al. 1989. 'Prevalence and Stability of Physical Aggression between Spouses: A Longitudinal Analysis', *Journal of Consulting and Clinical Psychology* 57: 263–8.

Organisation for Economic Co-operation and Development (OECD). 2001. *Society at a Glance: OECD Social Indicators 2001*. Paris: OECD.

———. 2002. *OECD Employment Outlook July 2002*. Paris: OECD.

———. 2005a. *OECD Employment Outlook 2005*. Paris: OECD.

———. 2005b. *Society at a Glance: OECD Social Indicators*. Paris: OECD.

———. 2007a. *Babies and Bosses: Reconciling Work and Family Life* (Volume 5): A Synthesis of findings for OECD Countries, available at http://www.oecd.org/els/social/family.

———. 2007b. *Society at a Glance: OECD Social Indicators, 2006*. Paris: OECD.

———. 2008a. *Growing Unequal?: Income Distribution and Poverty in OECD Countries*. Paris: OECD.

———. 2008b. *OECD Employment Outlook*. Paris: OECD.

———. 2009. *OECD Employment Outlook*. Paris: OECD.

Pahl, Jan. 1995. 'His Money, Her Money: Recent Research on Financial Organisation in Marriage', *Journal of Economic Psychology* 16: 361–76.

———. 2001. 'Couples and Their Money: Theory and Practice in Personal Finances', in R. Sykes, C. Bochel, and N. Ellison, eds, *Social Policy Review 13*. Bristol: Policy Press, 17–37.

———. 2005. 'Individualisation in Couple Finances: Who Pays for the Children?', *Social Policy and Society* 4, 4: 381–91.

————. 1992. *Women and Divorce in Canada: A Sociological Analysis*. Toronto: Canadian Scholars' Press.

————. 2002. *Fleeing the House of Horrors: Women Who Have Left Abusive Partners*. Toronto: University of Toronto Press.

Sharlin, S.A., F.W. Kaslow, and H. Hammerschmidt. 2000. *Together through Thick and Thin: A Multinational Picture of Long-Term Marriages*. New York: Haworth Clinical Practice Press.

Shorter, Edward. 1975. *The Making of the Modern Family*. New York: Basic Books.

Shriner, Michael. 2009. 'Marital Quality in Remarriage: A Review of Methods and Results', *Journal of Divorce and Remarriage* 50: 81–99.

Singh, S. 1997. *Marriage Money: The Social Shaping of Money in Marriage and Banking*. Sydney: Allen & Unwin.

Skolnick, A. 1987. *The Intimate Environment*, 4th edn. Toronto: Little, Brown.

Smart, Carol, and Bren Neale. 1999. *Family Fragments?* Cambridge: Polity Press.

————, and Selma Sevenjuijsen. 1989. *Child Custody and the Politics of Gender*. London: Routledge.

Smith, Marjorie. 2004. 'Relationships of Children in Stepfamilies with their Non-Resident Fathers', *Family Matters* 67 (Autumn): 28–35.

Smith, Raymond T. 1996. *The Matrifocal Family: Power, Pluralism and Politics*. New York: Routledge.

Smyth, Bruce. 2002. 'Research into Parent–Child Contact after Separation', *Family Matters* 62 (Winter): 33–7.

————, ed. 2004. *Parent–Child Contact and Post-Separation Parenting Arrangements*. Research Report #9. Melbourne: Australian Institute of Family Studies.

————, G. Sheehan, and B. Fehlberg. 2001. 'Patterns of Parenting after Divorce: A Benchmark Study', *Australian Journal of Family Law* 15, 2: 114–28.

————, and Ruth Weston. 2004. 'The Attitudes of Separated Mothers and Fathers to 50/50 Shared Care', *Family Matters* 67 (Autumn): 8–15.

Speirs, Carol, and Maureen Baker. 1994. 'Eligibility to Adopt: Models of "Suitable" Families in Legislation and Practice', *Canadian Social Work Review* 11, 1: 89–102.

Stanley, S.S., G.K. Rhoades, and H.J. Markham. 2006. 'Sliding versus Deciding: Inertia and the Premarital Cohabitation Effect', *Family Relations* 55 (Oct.): 499–509.

Statistics Canada. 2002a. '2001 Census: Marital Status, Common-law Status, Families and Households', *The Daily*, 22 Oct.

————. 2002b. 'Changing Conjugal Life in Canada', *The Daily*, 11 July.

————. 2003. 'Marriages', *The Daily*, 2 June.

————. 2006. 'Concept: Census Family', *Definitions of Concepts and Variables*. Available at http://www.statcan.gc.ca/concepts/definitions/cfamily-rfamille-eng.htm.

————. 2007a. '2006 Census of Population', available at http://www40.statcan.ca/l01/cst01/familil52a.htm; http://www12.statcan.ca/English/census06/analysis/farmhouse/tables/table1.htm.

————. 2007b. '2006 Census: Families, Marital Status, Households and Dwelling Characteristics', *The Daily* 12 September.

————. 2007c. 'Marriages, 2003'. CANSIM Table 101–1013. Ottawa: Statistics Canada.

————. 2007d. 'Family Portrait: Continuity and Change in Canadian Families and Households in 2006: National Portrait: Individuals'. Ottawa: Statistics Canada, available at http://www12.statcan.ca/english/census06/analysis/famhouse/ind3.cfm.

————. 2007e. *Report on the Demographic Situation in Canada: 2005 and 2006*. Ottawa: Statistics Canada, available at http://www.statcan.gc.ca/91–209-x/2004000/5200779-eng.htm.

————. 2008. 'Live Births, by Geography—Marital Status of Mother', Table 2.5, available at http://www.statcan.gc.ca/pub/84f0210x/2006000/5201681-eng.htm.

Statistics New Zealand. 2004. 'Family Types', available at http://www.stats.govt.nz/analytical-reports/looking-past-20th-century/changes-in-society/family-types.htm.

Strong-Boag, Veronica. 1982. 'Intruders in the Nursery: Childcare Professionals Reshape the Years One to Five, 1920–1940', in Joy Parr, ed., *Childhood and Family in Canadian History*. Toronto: McClelland & Stewart, 160–78.

Sweeney, Megan M. 2004. 'The Changing Importance of White Women's Economic Prospects for Assortative Mating', *Journal of Marriage and Family* 66, 4: 1015–28.

Swift, Karen. 1995. *Manufacturing 'Bad Mothers'? A Critical Perspective on Child Neglect*. Toronto: University of Toronto Press.

Synnott, Anthony. 1983. 'Little Angels, Little Devils: A Sociology of Children', *Canadian Review of Sociology and Anthropology* 20, 1: 79–95.

Taylor-Gooby, Peter, ed. 2004. *New Risks, New Welfare: The Transformation of the European Welfare State*. Oxford: Oxford University Press.

Tew, Marjorie. 1998. *Safer Childbirth? A Critical History of Maternity Care*, 3rd edn. London and New York: Free Association Books.

Thomas, Derrick. 2001. 'Evolving Family Living Arrangements of Canada's Immigrants', *Canadian Social Trends* (Summer): 16–22.

Thorne, Barry. 1982. 'Feminist Rethinking of the Family: An Overview', in Barry Thorne, with Marilyn Yalom, eds, *Rethinking the Family: Some Feminist Questions*. New York: Longman, 1–24.

Torjman, Sherri, and Ken Battle. 1999. *Good Work: Getting It and Keeping It*. Ottawa: Caledon Institute of Social Policy.

Tough, S., K. Tofflemire, K. Benzies, N. Fraser-Lee, and C. Newburn-Cook. 2007. 'Factors Influencing Childbearing Decision and Knowledge of Perinatal Risks Among Canadian Men and Women', *Maternal and Child Health Journal* 11: 189–98.

Trapski, Judge, et al. 1994. *The Child Support Review*. Wellington: New Zealand Parliament.

Tschann, Jeanne, Lauri Pasch, Elena Flores, Barbara Marin, E. Marco Baisch, and Charles Wibbelsman. 'Nonviolent Aspects of Interparental Conflict and Dating Violence Among Adolescents', *Journal of Family Issues* 30, 3: 295–319.

Turner, B.S. 1995. 'Aging and Identity', in M. Featherstone and A. Wernick, eds, *Images of Aging*. London: Routledge, 245–60.

Ungar, Michael. 2008. 'Resilience Across Cultures', *British Journal of Social Work* 38: 218–35.

United Nations (UN). 2000. *The World's Women: Trends and Statistics*. New York: UN.

United Nations Children's Fund (UNICEF). 2000. *A League Table of Child Poverty in Rich Nations*. Florence: Innocenti Research Centre.

———. 2003. *A League Table of Child Maltreatment Deaths in Rich Nations*. Florence: Innocenti Research Centre.

———. 2005. *Child Poverty in Rich Nations 2005*. Report Card #6. Florence: Innocenti Research Centre.

———. 2008. *The Child Care Transition*. Report Card #8. Florence: Innocenti Research Centre.

United States Department of Health and Human Services. 2002. 'Births: Final Data for 2001', *National Vital Statistics Reports* 51, 2: 1–103.

Ursel, Jane. 1992. *Private Lives, Public Policy: 100 Years of State Intervention in the Family*. Toronto: Women's Press.

Van den Berg, Axel, and Joseph Smucker, eds. 1997. *The Sociology of Labour Markets: Efficiency, Equity, Security*. Toronto: Prentice-Hall Allyn and Bacon Canada.

Vanier Institute of the Family (VIF). 1994. *Profiling Canada's Families*. Ottawa: VIF.

———. 2000. *Profiling Canada's Families II*. Ottawa: VIF.

———. 2004. *Profiling Canada's Families III*. Ottawa: VIF.

———. 2007. *Family Facts*. Ottawa: VIF, available at http://www.vifamily.ca/library/facts/facts.html.

———. 2008. 'Fertility Intentions: If, When and How Many?', *Fascinating Families*. Ottawa: VIF.

———. 2009. 'Becoming a "Lone-Mother"', *Fascinating Families*. Ottawa: VIF.

Van Laningham, J., D.R. Johnson, and P. Amato. 2001. 'Marital Happiness, Marital Duration and the U-shaped Curve: Evidence from a 5-Wave Panel Study', *Social Forces* 78, 4: 1313–41.

Veblen, T. 1953 [1899]. *The Theory of the Leisure Class*. New York: Mentor.

Veevers, Jean E. 1980. *Childless by Choice*. Toronto: Butterworths.

Vogler, C., and J. Pahl. 1994. 'Money, Power and Inequality within Marriage', *Sociological Review* 42: 263–88.

Voiçu, M., B. Voicu, and K. Strapcova. 2008. 'Housework and Gender Inequality in European Countries', *European Sociological Review* 21 September (online publication).

Vosko, Leah F. 2000. *Temporary Work: The Gendered Rise of a Precarious Employment Relationship*. Toronto: University of Toronto Press.

Wadsworth, J., I. Burnell, B. Taylor, and N. Butler. 1983. 'Family Type and Accidents in Preschool Children', *Journal of Epidemiology and Community Health* 37: 100–4.

Waite, Linda. 2005. 'Marriage, Family and Health', keynote address to the Australian Institute of Family Studies Conference, 9–11 Feb., Melbourne.

Walker, R., D. Turnbull, and C. Wilkinson. 2002. 'Strategies to Address Global Caesarean Section Rates: A Review of the Evidence', *Birth* 29 (1 Mar.).

Walker, Seb. 2005. 'Divorce Makes Women Happier Than Men', *The Guardian*, 5 July, available at http://www.guardian.co.uk.

Wall, Glenda. 2004. 'Is Your Child's Brain Potential Maximized? Mothering in an Age of New Brain Research', *Atlantis* 28, 2: 41–50.

———. 2005. 'Childhood and Child Rearing', in Baker (2005: 163–80).

———. 2009. 'Childhood and Child Rearing', in Baker (2009: 91–107).

———, and Stephanie Arnold. 2007. 'How Involved is Involved Fathering? An Exploration of the Contemporary Culture of Fatherhood', *Gender & Society* 21, 4: 508–27.

Wallace, P. 1999. *The Psychology of the Internet*. Cambridge: Cambridge University Press.

Wallerstein, J., and S. Blakeslee. 1996. *The Good Marriage*. New York: Warner Books.

Walsh, Rebecca. 2005. 'Obesity To Shorten Many Lives', *New Zealand Herald*, 19 Mar., 1.

Walsh, Sara. M. 2008. 'Kathleen A. Bogle, *Hooking up: Sex, Dating and Relationships*', *Journal of Youth and Adolescence* 37, 6, July.

Ward, Peter. 1990. *Courtship, Love, and Marriage in Nineteenth-Century English Canada*. Montreal and Kingston: McGill-Queen's University Press.

Weedon, J., M. Abrams, M. Green, and J. Sabini. 2006. 'Do High-Status People Really Have Fewer Children?' *Human Nature* 17, 4: 377–92.

Weeks, Jeffrey. 2002. 'Elective Families: Lesbian and Gay Life Experiments', in A. Carling, S. Duncan, and R. Edwards, eds, *Analysing Families*. London: Routledge, 218–28.

Weir, L. 1996. 'Recent Developments in the Governance of Pregnancy', *Economy and Society* 25, 3: 372–92.

Weston, Ruth, and Robyn Parker. 2002. 'Why Is the Fertility Rate Falling? A Discussion of the Literature', *Family Matters* 63 (Spring/Summer): 6–13.

———, Lixia Qu, Robyn Parker, and Michael Alexander. 2004. '"It's Not for Lack of Wanting Kids . . .": A Report on the Fertility Decision Making Project', Melbourne: Australian Institute of Family Studies, Research Report #11.

Whitehead, Margaret, Bo Burström, and Finn Diderichsen. 2000. 'Social Policies and the Pathways to Inequalities in Health: A Comparative Analysis of Lone Mothers in Britain and Sweden', *Social Science and Medicine* 50, 2: 255–70.

Whitehouse, E.R., and A. Zaidi. 2008. 'Socio-Economic Differences in Mortality', OECD Social Employment and Migration Working Papers # 71.

Whitty, Monica T. 2007. 'Revealing the "Real" Me, Searching for the "Actual" You: Presentations of Self on an Internet Dating Site', *Computers in Human Behaviour* 24, 4: 1707–23.

Willen, Helena, and Henry Montgomery. 1996. 'The Impact of Wish for Children and Having Children: Attainment and Importance of Life Values', *Journal of Comparative Family Studies* 27: 499–518.

Wilson, M., and M. Daly. 1994. *Spousal Homicide*. Ottawa: Canadian Centre for Justice Statistics.

Winch, Robert. 1955. 'The Theory of Complementary Needs in Mate Selection: A Test of One Kind of Complementariness', *American Sociological Review* 20 (Oct.): 552–5.

Winterich, Julie A. 2007. 'Aging, Femininity, and the Body: Appearance Changes Mean to Women with Age', *Gender Issues* 24: 51–69.

Wister, Andrew. 2005. *Baby Boomer Health Dynamics*. Toronto: University of Toronto Press.

Wolfe, David, and Peter Jaffe. 2001. 'Prevention of Domestic Violence: Emerging Initiatives', in S. Graham-Bermann and J. Edleson, eds, *Domestic Violence in the Lives of Children: The Future of Research, Intervention and Social Policy*. Washington: American Psychological Association.

———, Claire Crooks, Debbie Chiodo, and Peter Jaffe. 'Child Maltreatment, Bullying, Gender-Based Harassment, and Adolescent Dating Violence: Making the Connections', *Psychology of Women Quarterly* 33, 1: 21–4.

Woodward, Lianne, David M. Fergusson, and Jay Belsky. 2000. 'Timing of Parental Separation and Attachment to Parents in Adolescence: Results of a Prospective Study from Birth to Age 16', *Journal of Marriage and the Family* 62: 162–74.

World Health Organization (WHO). 1998. *The World Health Report 1998: Life in the Twenty-First Century: A Vision for All.* Geneva: WHO.

———, and UNICEF. 1990. *Innocenti Declaration on the Protection, Promotion and Support of Breastfeeding*, available at http://www.unicef.org.

Worrall, Jill. 2008. 'Kin Care—Understanding the Dynamics', *Social Work Now* December: 4–11.

Worth, H.B., and K.E. McMillan. 2004. 'Ill-Prepared for the Labour Market: Health Status in a Sample of Single Mothers on Welfare', *Social Policy Journal of New Zealand* 21 (Mar.): 83–97.

Wu, Zheng. 1996. 'Childbearing in Cohabitation Relationships', *Journal of Marriage and the Family* 58: 281–92.

———. 2000. *Cohabitation: An Alternative Form of Family Living.* Toronto: Oxford University Press.

———, and Christoph Schimmele. 2005. 'Divorce and Repartnering', in Baker (2005a: 202–28).

Zelizer, V. 1994. *The Social Meaning of Money.* New York: Basic Books.

Zhang, Xuelin. 2009. 'Earnings of Women With and Without Children', *Perspectives* (Mar.): 5–13.

Index

stepfamilies, 164–6; adolescents and, 111;
household money and, 128
structural functionalism, 18–20; gender
roles and, 119–20
structural theories, 18–20; dating and, 42,
47–8
Study of Stepchildren and Step-Parenting
(UK), 166
Supreme Court of Canada, 62
surnames: marriage and, 76
survey research, 26
symbolic interaction perspective, 22
systems theory, 20

tax: child support and, 159–60
Taylor-Gooby, Peter, 144–5
technology: future family life and,
192–4
telework, 191–2
time-use studies, 120–1
transportation: future family life and, 193
trousseaus, 74

Unemployment Insurance, 138, 141
Ungar, Michael, 104–5
United Nations, 93; Children's Fund
(UNICEF), 104, 106; Convention on
the Elimination of All Forms of
Discrimination against Women, 82

Veblen, Thorstein, 125
violence: dating and, 43–4; domestic, 80–2,
105; prevention of, 81

Waite, Linda, 79
Wall, Glenda, 97
Wallerstein, J., and S. Blakeslee, 178
war: marriage and, 39, 77
wealth accumulation, 125–7, 130–1
Weber, Max, 23
weddings, 67, 74–5
'wedfare programs', 191
welfare state: family policies and, 6–9;
see also liberal welfare state
Whitehead, Margaret, et al., 163
women: age at first birth and, 92;
child-bearing and, 93–4; 'child penalty'
and, 104, 136–7; earnings gap and,
136–7; legal rights and, 65–6; as
stay-at-home mothers, 102–3; veil and,
16–17; as widows, 73; see also gender
Woodward, Lianne, et al., 163–4
work/life balance/stress, 124, 192
World Health Organization (WHO), 99, 100

youth: see adolescence; children

'zero population growth', 93
Zhang, Xuelin, 104